Living on Love

Living on Love

Living on Love

"The Messenger"

Klaus J. Joehle

Writers Club Press
San Jose New York Lincoln Shanghai

Living on Love
"The Messenger"

Writers Club Press
an imprint of iUniverse.com, Inc.

For information address:
iUniverse.com, Inc.
5220 S 16th, Ste. 200
Lincoln, NE 68512
www.iuniverse.com

ISBN: 0-595-17287-3

Printed in the United States of America

To My Son,
Who stood by me?
I say this:
Anything and Everything
Is possible
With Love.

Children

The problem with our children is
That they have so much to teach us
But so little time to do it in.
My problem is it has taken me 15 years to learn that.
Now I fear that
I've missed most of my education.

Epigraph

What if after many years of studying so called ancient wisdom, you find yourself stuck? All the information is there but nothing seems to be working.

Then one day, out of work and out of money, you come up with a brainstorm.

You take all the information you learned about meditation, remote viewing, out of body travel, and so on. You decide to mentally travel into the future to see what the results of tomorrows sports lottery will be. But just as the money starts rolling in you run into your future self.

You ignore him!

So another future self comes to see you, to change the past or maybe to change the future.

What if your future self offered you information about Love that has been kept secret for centuries? Information that will make all your dreams come true. Would you let go of the easy money?

As you take this book home, so you will need to choose also.

Klaus J. Joehle

Contents

Foreword

You are about to embark on a journey most of us only dreamed possible in these tiny moments when we dared to dream the seemingly impossible hopes.

Over the last 30 years I read all the books, spent countless hours-meditating, visualizing, learning to travel out of my body but the whole time I felt like I was missing something. Also after a while all the books just seemed to be a rehash of the same material. Nothing new, at least that seemed to be making any real difference.

Some time in November of 1995 after getting laid off work and having no intention of looking for work, I went to visit a friend of mine who at the time was working on his sports bets. We were talking about the bets and how much money he wasn't making, when a thought occurred to me.

I looked at my friend and suggested that maybe a person could use their subconscious mind to see into the future and figure out who was going to win the game. He thought I was nuts and said that there was no way to predict the future, and he gave me about 20 reasons why it would not work. It's pretty obvious to me that he is a lot more thickheaded then I am. But the more I thought about it, the more I liked the idea. By the time I got home, I had it more or less worked out in my mind. I figured all I needed to do was to find a state of mind where the conscious and subconscious come together and worked together as one rather than being separate. It sounds simple and it was, even though it did take a while to work out the details and figure out a plan. I went back to the library and picked up a few more books. I played around with it for about a week or two, trying different things out. Anyway I took all the information I could find and mixed it all up, a little bit from here and a little bit from there. The conclusion that I came to was that I needed to be in a very deep meditating state, or a trance-like state of mind and then travel into the future to see the game results.

It worked and in no time at all I was in the money. I was making small bets and winning small amounts at a time. As time went by, I tried to get my friend to do the same thing. Figuring that this way we could compare answers and do even better, but he was scared and refused to have anything to do with it. I kept at him, but to no avail. Even though he was not even the least religious he kept saying that I might be breaking some cosmic law and may get more then I was bargaining for. Well as it turned out there is no such law in the universe, but it appears the Universe or All That There Is had its own plan. Totally unaware, I was walking right into it.

This is how it started but not how it ended. Even science is slowly realizing there is an invisible power we call Love. For centuries the word Love has been used to describe feelings and emotions but nothing has been said about this incredible power source that's responsible for sustaining all that is around us. Just imagine the life you could create if you know how to tap into this source. Just imagine the difference you could make in this world. The fact is that this source lies within all of us, we are born with it. For centuries the information has been passed down, to only a handful and I really mean only a handful. Trying to win the lottery has nothing to do with the information you are about to discover other than that it was the motivation that brought me to quiet my mind long enough for me to be shown something incredible that has been hidden right in front of us.

Sometimes I ask myself if the world is ready for this information? The only answer I get is from the many e-mails I have received and continue to receive. They are from people that are amazed at how incredible this information is and how easy and fast it works. I also worried whether or not it could be used wrongly or in a negative way, for it seems that some have tried it. Let this be a warning. Love Energy, for better wording is a conscious energy and is conscious of what you are trying to do. I speculate that this is why it works so well.

The story you are about to read is true to the best of my ability to write it and the information you will discover in this book to the best of my knowledge has never been written about before. Although the power of Love is mentioned in many writings nowhere is it explained how to use this Love energy to create the life and Love you are looking for.

If you're tired of reading the same rehashed material over and over and are ready to take the next step then read on. You'll discover a little known secret about Love that no one ever imagined possible. If you find yourself reading a lot of books or searching for something to take you further, then this is the information you have been searching for. This is what we all have been searching for.

All my Love
Klaus Joehle

Preface

A Controversial Note from the Author

This is my opinion, take what you like and leave the rest.

It seems for as long as we have been on this planet we have found a way to destroy ourselves. We go to war and kill others by the thousands. We attack those who seem weaker than us and take what they have. We will, and have killed others for what we want and have even been killed in the attempt. Half the world seems to be reasonably at peace while the other half is raging in war. Even when we try to help those that can not defend themselves against an aggressor we end up becoming like the aggressor that we are trying to stop. For centuries we have been taught that we do not have the power to stop an aggressor other than by fighting and killing. It has become a vicious circle. They're are those who desperately try to live in peace only to be attacked at sometime for what they have. We walk in fear of what others might do to us. We lock our doors lock our cars, install security alarms and all to no avail. There is another way. Here is an example.

The people that lived in my home before me were broken into and robbed five times in seven years. Five times their home was vandalized and their things taken from them. On the other hand I have lived here in peace and for a long time, even though my neighbor did not. I have no alarms; my doors and windows are never locked. My vehicles are not locked and my garage door is always open with all the tools just sitting there. OK maybe sitting under the rubble. Even when we go away everything stays unlocked and when we return not even a blade of grass has been disturbed. I have not even seen the keys for this house since I moved in. Most would agree that this is being foolish and just waiting for trouble. Normally I would agree but you have not seen the information in this book in action, nor what it is capable of.

At one time I was convinced like many others that God just placed us here and gave us no power to create heaven on earth. But in time I realized that it did not make sense. At the same time I did not know where the power was or how to access it.

To believe that God made us powerless to create heaven on earth and to believe that we are part of God and left powerless to stop those who want to destroy everything in their path, that's silly and there is no truth to it. The truth is we have the power to stop this and it lies inside of us waiting to be activated. The power that I'm speaking of is Love and we do not need to hurt those that would hurt us in order to stop them.

Don't let the word Love, nor the way it has been described fool you, that is exactly how it has been hidden from us. I am amazed how the word Love has been worked over to make a mountain look like a pimple. Most people would agree that Love is one of the most powerful forces in the universe but that is as far as it goes. We have been taught and in many ways have taught ourselves that Love is a feeling and an unattainable force but that is not true. There is much more to Love and what we can do with it. The best way to hide something is to make it look like nothing, silly and wishy-washy. The universe and all that you see is not a closed system nor is it a self-sustaining. It needs an outside source of energy and that is what we call Love. Think about it, whatever you believe created all of this also created us and in doing so also gave us the power to create heaven on earth. Does that not make sense?

Allot of people are scared of what tomorrow will bring for themselves and for their children.

I can't blame them but after you read this book you will agree that the only thing that's really scary is not having this information and to not be able to give it to our children.

I have learned to meditate and all kinds of wonderful things have come from our spiritual scientists from the east and Tibet. What always bothered me was the fact that after 500 years of meditating, Tibetans had to flee their country and leave their people to be enslaved, tortured and killed. I'm not trying to put them down I'm saying that something was missing along the way they and all of us missed something that could of at least kept us safe. If you can not keep yourself and your children safe while making the world a better place to live in, then there is something missing. Something is wrong with that picture. We are all waiting for God to come and straighten it all out, the fact is he gave us free will and he gave us the power to do it ourselves without hurting anyone or causing anyone harm. I know that saying this is a big statement but the proof is there, from the countless e-mail I get from people who have witnessed this same miracle, as I have.

I am not religious other than that I believe in something larger and more loving than myself.

When I was younger I was sent to Sunday school like most of you but I felt that there was something not complete. It's like this. When Jesus said to turn the other cheek something was left out. That something was send and fill them with Love because that will stop them in their tracks, and of course the instructions on how to send Love in a way that is affective. If turning the other cheek works so well on its own then when they robbed your store or robbed your house then why not give them more then what they were looking for? If it works so well why are churches locked? The point of turning the other cheek was to not hit back but there was a piece of information missing. How to work with Love and how to activate this incredible power source to not only protect yourself but to also change the very person that is threatening you or your life and to live the life you want without fear.

If you were in a place with no surface water and you had never seen a drilling rig then even if we all agreed that there is water we would still die of thirst. For if we do not know what a drilling rig is or how to use the rig, it would just sit there just like the Love inside of us. If Love is the most powerful force we know of. And if we can use it to change our lives, create the things we want, happiness, safety, Love, joy and so on, It is of no use if we do not know how to access it or where to get it.

If I was talking of anything other then Love it would scare me but Love has a consciousness of its own and will not do any harm. As you read on you will come to discover this for yourself and you will be amazed beyond words.

The information I write in this book you will not find anywhere else, but that will change quickly. When I first wrote this book I placed it onto a web page to see if people were interested and to see if it was understandable, for some things are hard to express in words. The response was over whelming. People wrote in saying this is the missing piece and they were amazed at the results. Thank You for all your support.

If you consider yourself what some call a light worker, or healer, or if your are at least trying to be one of these, this is the information you have been looking for. This is the information that will take you to your next step.

To the Tibetans I apologize if the example I made offends you but it is time to know how to release the Love energy this world so desperately needs.

This is for the two Tibetans who are of the few that know of this information and have held onto it tight. The time is now, one way or another it is time for people to know what loving power lies within them and it is time to release it.

It is time for people to be able to live in peace and without fear and to be able to create the life they want. It is fine what you have accomplished, that you have lived for a long time, and that you do not need to eat or drink water. That you at will can be invisible to the naked eye. But you have forgotten what it is like for those who have been convinced that they are powerless and are living under the fists of others. You may have had your reasons but in my mind and from what I have seen going on in the world they were not good enough to keep this to yourselves. That is where we bang heads and will continue to do so. But then you knew this was coming. I live well I live safe but it is time for others to be able to do so also.

For those that believe in a God, he gave you the power to create heaven on earth and if you use it he will come or perhaps in a second he/she will already be here. Think about this. Do you do everything for your children or do you give them the skills and abilities to do it themselves? If you are going to let this information go because it came from a nobody like myself instead of a high priest well that's up to you. You have the God given right and abilities to create the world that God wanted.

Take what you like and leave the rest for someone that will Love it. As it should be.

For those that have and continue to write me, I apologize that you will most likely receive only short notes back, because there is too much and too little time. All the information is here in this book. How I found the information, how to work with it, what to expect, and some of my own experiences. That is all I have to give you other than my Love. Take the information and run with it. In two years you will look back and be amazed at what you have accomplished. We will all be. In the next few pages I will try to answer some of the most asked questions. I hope that this will help?

All my Love to you on your journey!

Klaus J Joehle

Acknowledgements

To my sweetheart and wife
Who helped so much
Roberta Joehle

Lets fall in Love
Every moment, day, night, week, year

All my love
Klaus

Editorial Method

Spelling and Grammar?

Perfect spelling has never fed a hungry child.
Perfect grammar has never mended a broken heart
A finely pressed suit only hides the glow of love that is missing
A lack of love is the only imperfection I know
So get over it
The need for Perfect spelling and perfect grammar
Is boring, time consuming elusions that hide what is truly needed.
Thirty to fifty hours more editing would have made this perfect.
But instead it fed some starving children.
So I hope that each word and each sentence of imperfection
Reminds you of what's really important.

I did pay to have this book edited once and upon its return there were
still many errors.
After its return my wife took over and after many long hours of editing
and re-editing
She gave into one healthy fact of life
Nothing is Perfect
Or maybe it is
My wife believes everything is perfect in it's own special way…

Introduction

For centuries certain information about Love and the amount of power it gives you has been kept secret and hidden. That's all about to change. If you want to create the life you have dreamed about than read on.

In all honesty the last thing I wanted to do was become a writer, especially writing about Love. If it weren't for the amount of power and ability that Love gave me to create the life I wanted...I wouldn't even consider it. Using Love I have found that I can virtually instantly create everything I want. Using Love I have gained so much ability and power to create what I desire, that if it wasn't Love that I was using then it would almost be scary. My life has turned into a fairy tale and is beyond anything I have ever hoped possible for myself. I know that this sounds like a big statement to make. But it's quite true. Even my sweetheart who was open minded but also skeptical had little choice but to believe, because the Magic is an every day thing almost beyond words. The amount of personal power that Love gives you, not to control others but to create your life and your experiences is overwhelming. The beautiful thing about it is that it also seems always to work out the best for everyone in the end. After all if it wasn't all that great then it wouldn't have been kept a secret.

Working and creating with Love is very easy, there is a little knack to it, but extremely easy to learn. The list of what you can do with Love or perhaps I could say Love energy is endless. I could give you several hundred examples. You'll find quite a few examples in this book Living on Love "The Messenger". My favorite saying is Take what you like and leave the rest for someone that might Love it. The choice is yours.

All our Love to you on your journey and choices.

Klaus J. Joehle

Chapter One

It was early winter. Usually at this time of the year it is quite cold, but this year was warm, almost like summer. It was a very cloudy day, and it looked like it was going to rain.

I was at home trying to write this book, but I just could not figure out how to tell this story. I am not a writer and have never written a thing before. I tried for several hours to write, and even though I had made some rough outlines and notes of things that had happened, I still could not get any further than the first pages. I couldn't find the words to explain what had gone on two years ago that changed my life forever. Finally I gave up and decided to drive downtown to run some errands.

I parked my car in a place I knew I could leave it all afternoon without having to pay for parking or get a ticket, and walked to the various places I wanted to go. After I had done my running around, I decided to stop and see a friend of mine named Henry, and ask if he wanted to go for a drink.

It doesn't take much to twist Henry's arm and we were at the bar in no time at all. It's a small quiet bar called Hy's. After we were there for several hours I decided it was time to go home. When I stepped outside it was pouring rain which is very unusual for this time of year…not to mention that it very seldom rains this hard here in Calgary.

I knew I was going to get soaked so I quickly ran from one sheltered spot to another, not that it helped; it's just one of those weird things we do even though logically it makes no sense. It was already dark and with the rain it was hard to see. I was standing under a small shelter trying to get my bearings. As I looked around I realized I was standing on a small deck covered with a roof, almost like a house verandah. A small sign for Neena's Bar flashed in the window.

I didn't remember ever seeing this place before. The whole place was maybe only 15 feet wide. It almost looked like it had squeezed itself right between two giant brick buildings.

I stepped inside. Looking around, I saw that there seemed to be only two people in the place other than the bartender. To the right there was a very small bar about ten feet long. A woman with long curly blond hair was sitting at the bar, talking to the bartender. To the left one man wearing a hat was sitting at a table. I walked over to the bar and sat down one stool from the blond woman.

As I sat down, she turned and said, "Is it still raining outside?"

"Yes, harder then ever," I answered. A shiver went up my spine.

"What can I get you?" the bartender asked.

"Scotch and rocks."

I looked at my wet pants and thought that I should have stopped somewhere else. Hot chocolate would have been nice. As I glanced around I wondered why I had come in here. The place felt eerie.

"Get him the good stuff, Danny." The blond woman interrupted my thoughts.

"Okay," said the bartender.

With a sheepish grin, I thought, this is going to cost me.

"Don't worry about it, it's on the house," said the blond woman as if she heard my thoughts.

"Thanks," I said, pleasantly surprised. And briefly glancing at her, I thought I could count with one hand the amount of times I've heard that statement.

She was very beautiful, with long curly blond hair that looked like it was as soft as silk. I shyly glanced away and continued looking around at the surroundings, thinking this place feels strange but homey and safe at the same time.

The bartender put the glass of Scotch in front of me with no ice in it. I was going to say something, but he was still holding onto the glass.

"We don't have hot chocolate, but I can heat this up for you!" he said quickly.

"Hot Scotch, never heard of it!" I frowned at him.

"It's quite good, try it," said the blond woman.

"Well, why not?" I was always willing to try something new.

My hair was wet and the water was dripping down my face. I was just going to ask where the washroom was when the bartender handed me a towel.

"Thanks."

I wiped my hair and face and as I put down the towel, I noticed out of the corner of my eye that the blond woman had moved to the chair next to me. That made me a bit nervous. I didn't look at her, but watched the bartender heat up my Scotch and waited for him to bring it back. The bar was ghostly quiet; no music was playing, no radio, not a sound, which is very unusual. This had the makings of another weird night. I thought to myself.

The bartender put down my glass of hot scotch in front of me and stood back waiting. I lifted the glass knowing that there were four eyes staring at me, and I took a sip.

I turned towards the blond woman. "Boy, it evaporates before it even hits your stomach! It's quite good, thank you."

We made eye contact about the same time that she smiled, and that was a mistake. Her eyes were like a calm ocean reflecting the moon and all the stars. I looked away, embarrassed. Danny was standing a few feet away washing some glasses. I sat in silence, staring forward and warming my hands on my glass of hot scotch. The quiet caused my mind to go back to my book. Maybe I should take a course, I thought to myself, or better yet, maybe I should forget the whole thing. That thought gave me a temporary feeling of relief.

"By the way, my name is Neena." The blond woman smiled.

I almost spilled my scotch. I tend to be a deep thinker and need to be brought back gently.

"Sorry, I didn't mean to scare you." Neena held out her hand.

"It's okay, I'm Klaus."

"Nice to meet you, Klaus. This good looking gentleman behind the bar is Danny."

"So why the big frown?"

"I didn't realize I was frowning"

"Girl friend problems?"

"No," I sipped my warm scotch.

"You might as well tell her, she won't quit until you do." Danny grinned from behind the bar.

"It's a long story," I said, shaking my head.

Neena leaned forward and gave me one of those 'we've got all night' looks. I nervously took another big sip of my scotch.

"Bring Klaus another one, Danny," said Neena.

"Actually, I really should go home," I said out loud, while another part of me said more please! There definitely is a lush in there somewhere.

Danny paid no attention to what I said and began pouring another drink.

"Come on, spill your guts, Klaus! Let's have it," Neena demanded, almost putting her face in mine to get me to make eye contact.

Part of me said, look at her, you big chicken.

"Klaus!" said Neena loudly.

I felt a fist hit my arm, interrupting my inner thoughts.

"What?" I was a little annoyed at being punched by a stranger.

"Come on, out with it!" she commanded.

Looking at her eyes, I wondered how many swords had been drawn to fight over those eyes. My lips began to move even ahead of my thoughts. I hate it when that happens.

"I'm trying to write a book about something that happened a while back, but I have no idea how to write it or even where to begin. It's way over my head," I said vowing to myself never to look in those eyes again.

"What's it about?" she asked, as Danny put my drink in front of me.

"It's about angels, sort of more about Love, I guess; about life, the reason for living, mostly about Love, I think..." I wished I had stopped somewhere else.

"Now that's interesting. So what happened?" Neena was definitely very persistent.

I shook my head. "It's a long story, and it's really bizarre."

Danny laughed. "If you make it out of here without telling her this story, that will be bizarre."

I shook my head again. "I wouldn't even know where to start."

I thought about it for a minute because in some way, I was itching to tell somebody. Considering that I would probably never see these people again, this was probably the perfect opportunity, but where would I start?

"Start at the very beginning," Neena brought me back from my thoughts.

Danny was leaning forward and ready to listen. He was obviously enjoying this.

"I have to tell you, it's a very strange story," I said.

"We're all ears." Neena was gleaming from her victory.

I can see that, I thought to myself.

"Give me a moment to collect my thoughts," I said.

Truth

What is imagination?
What is reality?
What is truth?
Is reality what we imagine?
Or is that
Which we imagine
Reality?
Then what is truth?

Chapter Two

"Does a story really have a beginning or even have an end? Where does it begin and where does it end? Does it begin at the start of a trip, the end of a trip..."

I stopped for a second to see if they were still with me.

"Or does it start when we made certain decisions which lead us to the path that led to the start of the story? Or does a story start when we leave for the journey, or when we start packing, or when we make the plans? And when does it end? If a story has changed us, does it end when we stop talking about it? And what is the important part? All the decisions that were made or the paths that were followed, a story is like the point where four roads meet? Let's face it...there is no beginning and no end."

If you ever want to get rid of someone, just give them a line like that...it will blow them away like dry leaves in the summer wind. I was looking at both of them, trying to hold back the smile that was building in me from the anticipation of watching them blow in the wind.

"I agree totally," said Danny. Neena nodded her head in agreement.

"It's sort of like truth. What is truth? Sometimes truth can be really puzzling," answered Neena. Obviously she was not blowing in the wind.

"What do you mean?" I asked, quite surprised that this might turn into a conversation.

"For instance, "she said, "ten people watch an accident happen. There are ten versions of what had happened and the only thing we know for sure is that there are several cars smashed. And then there is the question when did it really happen? Did it start when one car went out of control or did it start when the drivers got into their cars? They say our thoughts create our reality, and if that's so, then when did this accident really start?"

Danny and I both nodded our heads in agreement.

"Take that wallpaper over there," Danny noted. "We all see it, but is it the truth? What we see are colors and stripes; what we don't see are the people that work at the factories, making this paper, their fears, and their dreams. Nor do we see the trees that the paper came from and the people that built the wall, hoping to be able to feed their families, nor the owner hoping to make enough money to pay for all of this. All we see is colors and stripes. But that's not really the truth."

During the silence that followed, I took another sip of my scotch. I don't know why, but a dream I've had since I was a small child came to my mind. I was thinking about it when Neena interrupted my thoughts.

"There's that frown again." Neena nudged me with her elbow. I must have been feeling safe because my lips started to speak again without my total consent.

"I was just thinking of a dream I had when I was a kid. I believed that the world could be one big garden. You know what I mean, cities built in and around gardens, where everybody is happy, playing, planting fruit trees, flowers, berry bushes, and picking fruit. Playing with the wild life, animals like deer and rabbits and foxes running around not afraid of humans but drawn to them. People not afraid of people. Everyone caring for each other instead of beating each other down." I gestured with my hands. "Just a stupid dream, like anybody will ever see that happen, we're too busy blowing everything up and trying to make more money than our neighbors…"

"You never know!" Danny reached under the bar and brought out a strange green bottle. I saw it had a cork in it but no label.

"I've been saving this for a special occasion," Danny said with a strange gleam in his eye.

I looked at the bottle. "Where did you get that from, a pirate ship?"

Danny set down three glasses in a row and smiled. "No, not quite."

"It looks old," I said, as Danny tried to pull the cork.

"It is." Neena answered. "Very old!"

"What is it?"

They looked at each other for a moment, and Danny started to pour.

I shrugged my shoulders. "Okay then, what's the special occasion?"

I don't know if it was the scotch or the company, but I felt at ease and safe, even though they didn't answer my question. There was only enough in the bottle to fill three glasses half full. Danny put the empty bottle back under the bar and handed each of us a glass. It was thick and a dark blood-red color. I held it to my nose. It smelled sweet but had no scent of alcohol.

"It doesn't have any alcohol," Neena said.

I smiled. "What will we drink to?"

"To dreams. May they be beautiful and come true." Neena raised her glass.

"Here, here!" Danny sounded like a pirate.

It was incredible. It tasted like berries, sweet and thick, but I could not tell what kind of berry it was made of. My taste buds just came alive. I took another sip and another, and slipped into a world of my own. It felt like every cell in my body had sprung to life. The lush in me took over and by the time Neena said "you might want to take it slow!" it was too late. I was already sucking up the last drop and looking for more.

By the time I put down my glass both of them were laughing very hard. Looking at the other glasses I realized that they had only sipped theirs. It must have been the way I looked at Neena's glass that made her move it further away from my reach. I had no choice but to laugh with them. My mind was as clear as a bell. I also felt very energized.

"Wow! That's good stuff! I'll take a case…"

They were still laughing.

"Man, I feel like I could hog tie a dinosaur."

I'm pretty sure I had a grin on my face that would have been the envy of any clown.

Neena put her hand on mine. "So now that you know we're not going to ridicule you, maybe you would like to tell us this story about angels and Love."

"All right," I said, "fair's fair."

"Start from the beginning and don't leave anything out." she said.

"Just let me get my bearings," I slid my empty Scotch glass towards Danny so he could refresh it.

Just the way it is

The world is one big bowl of soup
Spinning around
And if peas and carrots
don't like each other
That's too bad.
Because they're sure going
to see a lot of each other
And nobody is leaving until
We are all nice and tender
That's just the way it is

Chapter Three

As Danny finished pouring my drink, I collected my thoughts. I reached in my coat pocket for my cigarettes. I glanced around to see if the gentleman was still sitting at his table. It looked like he had not moved an inch, rather odd especially since he hadn't been served the whole time I was there, and that had been almost an hour.

Danny put my drink in front of me while I took a drag of my cigarette.

"So, Klaus," Danny had a smirk on his face. "Am I pronouncing your name right?"

"Close enough." I stirred the ice in my glass.

"I figured you might want a cold one this time." Danny was still grinning.

"Your instincts were right. Thank you!" I grinned back.

"So how about that story?"

"I spent most of my life, except for the last couple of years, very unhappily. It's hard to explain but there has been a deep inner sadness. Actually a better way to explain it is that there seemed to be no happiness in me. Perhaps I should say happiness was just missing and no matter what happened, good or bad, it just was not there, and I could not do anything about it."

"You see, this is the problem…to really understand what I mean you need to know the rest of the story but at the same time I can't really tell you the story without telling you this part." I shook my head.

Danny came around the bar to grab a barstool, carried it to where he had been standing, and sat down.

"I can see the feelings, Klaus, but I can't hear them," Neena said.

"Just thinking about those days makes me feel a little sad," I said, in a low voice.

"Didn't people notice you were sad?" Neena's sympathetic voice was trying to help me along.

"That part really doesn't matter," I said. "But as far as the unhappiness goes, I tried all sorts of things over the years. I even watched other people to see what brought them happiness and then tried the same things. For instance, I noticed that when people purchased a new car they would be really happy...at least for a while. Or they'd act happy if they were getting into a relationship. There's an endless amount of things people do to be happy, and I basically tried them all. It may sound strange but none of these things did anything for me. As a matter of fact, a lot of the time it made me more miserable than I was before, simply because I was waiting for something to happen and nothing did. One crazy example comes to mind. I remember buying a new car, thinking that this would bring me happiness, but after I bought the car, I ended up sitting in it for two or three hours waiting for happiness or joy to flow over me like it seems to do for other people. But nothing happened. I was not any happier than before I bought the car. Yet it appears that this is not the case with other people. But I did not stop trying. I tried many other things over the years. I've read hundreds of books of all kinds from meditation to mind power, mind control, thinking positive, books on Love, books on life, all kinds of self-help books, but nothing helped. It was like there was something missing in me. But I also noticed that I was not the only one, there were lots of other people in much the same situation. Knowing that I was not the only one really didn't help much. In one way I was determined to solve this problem yet in another way I felt hopeless and many times gave up. I also took courses, and joined some self help groups. The most interesting of all was when I decided to go for ther-apy. It was a sad time for me, and I was convinced that there was some-thing wrong with me. But after three weeks of spilling my guts, I was told that I was fine and most definitely still sane, which was good to hear, and I was also told that there was no reason to continue with the sessions. All I needed to do was find something that I really enjoyed doing, and go for it. It's too bad that it was not quite that easy."

I stopped for a moment to light another cigarette when I noticed Danny was chuckling to himself.

"So what's so amusing to you about all of this?"

"I have never actually met someone before who would sit in a car for two or three hours waiting for happiness to spring up. But I salute your determination." Danny gave me a salute and a big grin.

"Then this unhappiness was your driving force?" Neena asked.

"Exactly. Instead of searching for money, fame, Love, career, or any of the normal things that people spend their lives trying to achieve, all I wanted was to be happy. Another way of saying it would be that I wanted to be free of the pain and the grief it was causing me."

I fell into deep thought as I watched the smoke curl upwards from my cigarette. I thought about some of the things that a lack of happiness makes you do and some of the paths that it leads you down. There was also something else on my mind and I was trying to decide whether or not I should say anything about it, when Neena interrupted my thoughts.

"It would be surprising if you had never thought of ending it all, or perhaps making an attempt!" she said.

I looked at Neena. Seeing the sparkles in her eyes, I thought obviously the universe has brought some of its best players into this game and is leaving nothing to chance. It appears that the universe knows me better than I was aware of.

I stood up and asked where the washroom was. I wanted a moment to collect my thoughts. Danny pointed to a small wooden plank door at the end of the bar.

The washroom was not very big, not much bigger than an outhouse with no windows and definitely no way to escape, if a person was so inclined. I thought about everything that I had said so far and decided to continue. After all, I had nothing to lose.

Life

Sometimes life is like
A giant poker game
That just goes on and on
And when we get really good at it
Then the universe might throw us a curve
Just to make us think
Maybe it can get even better
And so,
The game goes on.

Chapter Four

When I came out of the washroom I saw that the man at the table was still there. As I walked back to the bar, I kept my distance from him. One very important rule to remember when playing with the universe is that you need to play with respect, and preferably show respect; it's not that the universe will get upset at you, just that it might deal you a new card, because the universe also likes to teach. One of the things you do not want the universe to teach you is how to respect the game, believe me; I've been there and done that.

I sat on my barstool and drank the last of my scotch in one swallow. As I lit another cigarette I checked to make sure I had enough cigarettes to last, because it was going to be a long night.

Danny was pouring some orange juice in two glasses and asked if I would like the same. I hadn't noticed it before but apparently Neena and Danny had finished drinking whatever it was that had come out of that little green bottle.

"Yes, please! That's a really good idea." I said.

Danny put one glass of orange juice in front of me and one in front of Neena and sat down on his stool. There was a moment of silence.

"I guess I might as well tell you everything," I said with a slight hesitation. "In all, there were three times that I had decided to end it. They weren't really physical attempts, but nevertheless it was enough to cause quite the commotion."

"Are you sure you want to me to tell you this part or do you want me to skip over it?"

"Did anything interesting happen during those times?" asked Danny.

"Oh, most definitely!" I said, sarcastically. "My life has been one big song and dance."

"This should be interesting!" Neena looked at Danny as they both chuckled. I ignored them.

"Well, the first time was quite a few years ago. Things were actually not that bad except that I was unhappy. I had everything that should make a person happy, but that was not the case. The problem that got me so depressed at that time was that I had spent several months reading a few books and trying to make a very serious attempt at being happy. I had put a lot of effort in it, but had zero results. I felt like it was getting worse rather than better, and the straw that finally broke the camel's back came one night when I was reading a new book I had just picked up earlier that day. In this book, the person who wrote it described meeting some great teacher who taught him various fascinating things. What really upset me was that this person had some magical teacher come to him out of the blue and teach him all he wanted to know, while I have to struggle with my problems on my own. The other part that upset me was that he told about certain interesting things that he learned but did not give the instructions on how to do it. What's the point of telling me these things without giving me instructions? A waste of paper and a waste of my time." I leaned over towards Neena, and whispered, "My attitude at that time had bottomed out a bit."

I shook my head. "I remember it all, really clearly. I felt that the universe had forgotten about me. I was so frustrated and mad that I threw the book against the wall, and in my mind I screamed that if I didn't get some help right away, tomorrow morning I was going to take my car to the mountains and drive it over the cliff. I could feel the anger flowing through my veins. In the long run, I probably would not have done it but at that moment in my mind the decision was made. I figured that as long as I was here the universe could ignore me, but when I'm no longer here and standing in front of it, it's going to be a lot more difficult to ignore me then!"

"I don't know how long it was exactly, but I would say that no more than five minutes after I had screamed those words in my mind, it started. My inner senses just seemed to spring to life and I could feel something very big. It was huge and it seemed to be trying to squeeze itself into my apartment but it was just too big, and ended up taking up space in the entire apartment block, and even that was not enough. I really couldn't see anything, nor hear anything, but I could feel it with my whole being, that's the only way that I can describe it. I can't tell you how scared I was. I don't think I've ever been that scared. I almost peed my bed."

"I had a small but open apartment, and from my bed I could see the hallway, part of the kitchen, and a large part of my living room, All the lights were on because I don't like the dark. As soon as it gets dark, I've always felt like there is something big standing behind me, watching me. The dark has scared me for as long as I can remember. So I always keep the lights on, I don't even like dark corners, who knows what might be lurking in there? Within a few seconds, the lights started to flash on and off. It was almost musical. I was literally shaking with fear. I could feel and sense this presence forming and all of a sudden, I heard a voice in my head. It said, loudly and firmly, "You should know better…!"

"And that was it. The lights stopped blinking and whatever it was left. I was so scared that even though I needed to go to the washroom really badly, I did not leave my bed until the next morning. Nor did I sleep in my apartment the next night. The weird part was that there was a strange hush that came over the entire apartment building and stayed for several weeks. I heard two other people talking in the laundry room several days later, and apparently other people in the apartment building had also sensed something, but could not explain what it was."

"This whole incident was enough to keep me from whining about my circumstances for almost two years. But then it started to wear off."

I stopped to take another drink of my orange juice.

"What did you think it was that came to visit you?" Neena asked.

I shook my head. "I don't know, and I really don't want to know! Obviously I pissed somebody off, and frankly I just want to leave it at that because whoever came to visit was not in a good mood."

"Time passed and things did not improve. Actually, things began to deteriorate even more and it was becoming more and more difficult for me to fake it. Putting a smile on your face and pretending to be happy when you're not uses up an enormous amount of energy. Besides, it really scared the heck out of me, but in a strange way, I was prepared for the second time, and I was not going to just lay there shivering with fear. I planned on putting up a fight. After all, I have a right to be happy. When you're really depressed and down you usually don't think straight. And the bottom line is, I asked for help and didn't receive any."

I thought about what I had said for a minute. "Actually, that's not totally true," I said with a smirk.

"Oh, so you did get some help, then?" Neena asked.

"Yes. I won a trip to Mexico and while I was there, I met someone who could probably have helped me, but there were some strings attached and I just was not ready for it. But on the other hand, my path in life would have changed and perhaps I would never have had the opportunity to figure out how to win the lottery. And in some way that alone was almost worth it. Also, it might have meant that the story that I'm going to tell you would probably not have happened and that would be a big loss."

"Wait a minute! Are you trying to tell me that you figured out how to win the lottery?" Danny crossed his arms over his chest as if trying to tell me that such a thing was impossible.

"Yes, but we'll get to that later."

"Did you win more than once?" His eyes were as big as watermelons.

"Oh yeah." I pushed my chair away from the bar and stood up. I needed to stretch a bit.

"So did you get your butt kicked the second time around?" Neena smirked.

"No, not really. Quite the opposite, Don't you have any music?" I said, trying to change the subject. "It's too quiet in here!"

Danny stood up and walked over to a small tape player that was sitting on one of the shelves. He inserted a tape and adjusted the volume. I don't know what it was but it sounded like some kind of new age music that covered the silence nicely.

Home

Home, the next place I rest my soul
The crossroads of life
Where to plant some seeds of faith
Grow some crops of Love
And ponder which path to take next
Before heading Home
To the next crossroads of life
Where to plant some...

Chapter Five

I stretched a bit and sat down on my stool, planning on taking a break and listening to some music for a bit, but Danny gave me a look of impatience and tapped his fingers on the bar. I took the hint.

"It was roughly about two years later. Emotionally I was in the same place as before, only this time I had lost my job and was heading for my first bankruptcy. Losing my job or going into bankruptcy wasn't the worst of it. I had been working very hard for about one year in a support group and the only results that came from all the work was that I made some friends and got to whine a bit. Actually I got a few things off my chest but I still was not happy."

"So did you try anything else over those two years, other than the support group?" Neena asked.

"I tried lots of different things, but in one way or another it almost felt like something was stopping me from finding happiness. At that time nothing really made sense. I understand it now but back then, it was driving me nuts."

Everyone fell into silence. My mind was caught up in the past.

"I remember now. I was really upset. I was getting mad, you know? I was mad at the universe. In a lot of ways I was upset at whatever had come and visited me. What right did this thing have to scare me half to death but at the same time not really helping, just telling me I should know better? How am

I supposed know better? I was ready for a fight! I was also very tired of life. Nothing seemed to work for me and everything I touched seemed to turn to dust. I guess the best way to describe it would be to say that without happiness life just becomes an endless night. There was also an enormous deep inner pain that I just couldn't get rid of. It's nearly impossible for me to verbally express all the feelings and emotions that had at that time. I just couldn't understand why something like inner happiness, something that is supposed to be very natural would be so difficult for me to get, and it was driving me up the wall. I can get very cranky when I don't get what I want, especially if I work really hard for it. I should mention that I wasn't always totally unhappy. I had happy moments but I wasn't satisfied with the amount of happiness I had and I wanted more. Do you understand what I mean? "

Neena looked at me. "Yes, I think I understand."

"Did you really think that you could win with something that's perhaps a hundred times your size?" Danny asked.

I shook my head. "Winning is not always important. What is important is making the stand. Obviously the stand I was making wasn't exactly the right one. I just thought that life had nothing to offer me and I wanted to go somewhere else. What has always amazed me is that people will fight for rocks, dirt, and everything else except for Love and joy. Those are really the things that are worth fighting for. Everything else is nothing more than temporary."

Danny nodded in agreement.

"It was about one o'clock in the morning. I had made my decision that in the morning, I would simply drive to the mountains and make it look like an accident. But shortly after I made up my mind, I started to feel really peaceful. It was something I had never felt before. I was just lying there peacefully on my bed. I guess during that time I must have dozed off into a half-sleep and half-awake kind of state, and in that trance-like state I had a vision. It was as real as anything was, just like I was there physically. I was standing in the middle of an art gallery. I was looking around when I noticed that a lot of the pictures that were hanging on the walls were actually mine. That's when the fun began. I heard a door open and a woman walked in. She was tall and slim, with straight blond hair almost down to her shoulders, milky white skin, and large eyes. Before I knew it, she was standing directly in front of me. She was incredibly beautiful. The only way I can say it is to say she was more beautiful than her features. You could see the beauty even though it went beyond appearance. We were standing face to face no more than one foot apart."

She asked, "Are you Klaus?"

"The second she said that, it felt like every cell in my body had come to life and was paying attention. It was like I was made up of billions and billions of cells and each one had their own consciousness and at that very moment each one was paying attention. It was the weirdest feeling but at the same time one the most beautiful things I have ever experienced. It was like every cell in my body was an individual that had a stake in my life. They were almost like little beings, all working together to create my physical body so that I can live and experience physical life. I got the impression that everything I do affects them and matters to them. I tried to answer her question but I couldn't. There was too much going on in my body, so I just nodded my head. She put out her hand and as we shook hands, she said, "I would like you to stick around for awhile. It will all made sense later."

"Her voice was like listening to a thousand angels. Every cell in my body was still paying attention. It was overwhelming. Unfortunately, the second she stopped talking it was over, and I was back in my bed, wide-awake. Over the next few months I became obsessed with this vision and tried to go there many times, but with no success. Not even close."

"What was it that obsessed you so much about this vision?" Neena asked.

"I thought that maybe I would meet this person in real life. It was a silly idea, but a flicker of hope nevertheless. The hope alone kept me going for almost three years, a long three years I might add. But I think that was the plan. The universe probably figured that if it couldn't scare me into sticking around then seducing me might work better. Obviously it worked at least for a while."

"Maybe it was a chemical imbalance in your body. Did you ever think of that?" Danny asked.

"Oh, yeah. I thought about that, and even saw several doctors, but the bottom line is that I would rather suffer than be on some kind of drugs for the rest of my life. Most of them have serious side effects, and I was also afraid that some of the drugs might cause me in some way never to be happy without them. I also had some hope that someday I would find the answer. Drugs are only a temporary solution; they do not solve the problem or the issue that is really causing the problem in the first place. As far as I am concerned happiness and Love should not have anything to do with circumstances or experiences or my physical body."

The Last Stand

"Oh, my, aren't we the stubborn one?
Oh yes we are.
The universe you would stand against,
A thousand warriors, swords of steel drawn,
Five hundred heavy horses,
Against them you would stand with your dagger of straw
I have been a warrior forever and a day
And I do not know everything,
But this I know:
The blood will run this day
It will be yours my friend
And also mine.
For with honor I must stay.
So I ask you
Think
Is this a good day to die?

Chapter Six

"I'm pretty sure that it was close to three years later. It was early in the evening. I had gone out for dinner but couldn't eat. I was totally down and depressed, basically in tears. I got into my car and started driving. I was so numb and exhausted that I just headed down the highway towards the mountains. For some reason the feeling or knowing that within one or two hours it would all be over gave me a sense of relief."

"That's the problem with suicide: people think it's a way out, but actually it just starts the whole process again," Neena observed.

"I agree. But when you're down far enough, nothing matters anymore, other than to be free of that darkness even for a short while. I would have given anything just to be happy for a week. That's just the way it was."

Neena nodded her head sympathetically.

"Somewhere along the way you must have changed your mind, otherwise you wouldn't be here today," said Danny.

I don't know why, but for some reason Danny's upper lip was quivering. I thought that was rather amusing.

"Actually, I didn't change my mind. It's like this. About 30 minutes out of Calgary there used to be a gas station. I had plenty of gas in my car, but for some strange reason, as soon as I passed that gas station my engine sputtered and jerked. It would barely drive five miles an hour. It was like someone was turning the motor on and off really fast. I looked at my gas gauge and there was plenty of gas. Also it was a new car. I decided to cross the highway and head back to the gas station, figuring that maybe there was something wrong with the electronic ignition. But as soon as I got near the gas station, the car started to run perfectly. There was no point in trying to repair it, I thought, as long it would make the trip. After that, it really doesn't matter anymore. So I decided to cross the highway again in order to head back to the mountains."

"I had to drive about a mile down the highway before I found a place to cross over. I was in such a bad mood that I didn't even care if I had to push the car there. I crossed the highway and headed back towards the mountains. But as soon as I reached the gas station again the car began to sputter and jerk! I tried shifting the gears, turning the lights and the ignition on and off, but nothing seemed to help. The car sputtered along until I came to another highway crossing. The way the car was running I barely made it across. It took about 10 to 15 minutes to get back to the gas station because the car was running so poorly. The motor stalled a couple of times, but I got it started again. As soon as I got near the gas station, the motor came back to life and was running perfectly. So I passed the gas station and drove to the highway crossing, about a mile down. The car was still running fine. I crossed the highway and started heading back towards the mountains again. The stupid car ran fine until I was close to the gas station, then the same thing happened. The motor started to sputter and turn on and off. I was really getting very frustrated and decided to just keep driving the way it was, but the further away from the gas station I got, the worse the car was running. Finally, I had no choice but to cross the highway again, and sure enough as soon as I reached the gas station the car ran fine. It just sprang to life and purred like a kitten."

"Why didn't you stop at the gas station and have someone check it out?" Danny asked.

"It was about nine or ten at night, and I didn't think that there would be a mechanic there at that time. Besides it was running fine on the other side of the highway and in some way I knew that there was nothing wrong with the car. I wasn't going to let the universe stop me that easily, not this time."

"Talk about stubborn." Neena shook her head.

"Maybe, but I was mad, and I was going to show the universe that I've had enough."

"Let me guess. You kept this up until your car fell apart." Danny grinned as if he knew better.

"Something like that, but not quite." I said, "But I did keep going around in circles until about 9 or 10 the next morning."

They broke out in laughter. I had no choice but to join them. Looking back at this now, it seemed insane. And it probably was.

"You mean you finally gave up?" Neena carefully wiped the tears from her cheeks.

"No, I didn't really give up. It's more like I was exhausted and I decided to go to the gas station and have something to eat and gas up. Then I was going to continue. It's a good thing that they had an all night restaurant. I drove to the gas station and had the man fill up my tank. I remember that the attendant gave me a strange look, but I didn't pay much attention to it. I parked the car and went inside the restaurant. It was very quiet. There was only a couple of old truck drivers sitting at the main counter. So I took a seat in a small booth. I guess by that time I was almost delirious. I must have looked like hell. My face was probably drooping, my eyes bloodshot and my cheeks stained with tears. The waitress came over with a coffee mug and took one look at me, and with a very humorous and concerned look asked if I was the one that had been driving his car back and forth all night."

They were still laughing. While reaching for my cigarette, I showed them my best frown, but that just made them laugh even harder.

"Oh yeah, you go ahead and laugh! Some day the shoe will be on the other foot…then we'll see what's so funny."

"What do you think the odds are of that ever happening?" Danny looked at Neena.

She threw her hands in the air. "A million to one, maybe."

"To make a long story short, I told the waitress that my car wouldn't drive to the mountains, it would only drive back to Calgary. I could hardly speak. My mouth was dry and my lips were numb, and I was too tired to be embarrassed."

"She asked me where I was heading. And with a straight face, I said "Off a cliff!""

"She just stared at me. Then suddenly, she broke out in laughter. Finally she seemed to get hold of herself and leaned forward. 'You're a little thickheaded, aren't you? I'll get you some breakfast because you're going to be with us for a long time.'"

"She poured some coffee into my cup and headed for the kitchen. I expected to hear some laughter from the kitchen but heard nothing. I assumed that she didn't tell anyone."

"She never asked me why I was trying to drive over a cliff, but after a few more words, some free coffee and free breakfast, I got into my car and headed home."

By this time both of them were laughing so hard that it was starting to tick me off, and I excused myself and went to the washroom. I wasn't really upset at them, just a little (or maybe allot) embarrassed.

Today this gas station is closed; nothing is left but an abandoned building. I still go there sometimes and wonder how many others like me had stopped there.

Well here I am today, and happy for it. As far as the promise that it would all make sense at the end, that came true. But as far as knowing better is concerned, I'm still a little bit ticked about that one.

And to the very kind and generous waitress: Thank you!

Wanted

One Guardian Angel.
Must possess an incredible,
Unimaginable and totally
Inconceivable patience.
Send Resume and Lottery Ticket
To Box 40081
Attention Klaus.

Chapter Seven

By the time I came back from the washroom, Neena and Danny had pulled themselves together again, but they were still grinning. As I sat down on my stool, Danny asked if I wanted some more orange juice.

"We didn't mean to laugh at you like that," Neena said.

"You have to admit the part about being thick-headed was pretty funny," added Danny.

"I guess you've got me there." I nodded my head in agreement.

"So is that it?" she asked.

"No, not even close! From here on it gets really wacky."

Danny sat on his stool. "Well, the night is still young. We're ready whenever you are."

Danny's top lip began to quiver again for a moment. I leaned over towards Neena. "Why does Danny's lip quiver every once in a while?"

"Whenever he's holding something back. He doesn't make a good poker player." she laughed.

For a moment I wondered what Danny might be holding back. Somehow the whole thing didn't quite sit well with me. I always like to keep my eyes and ears open for things that are slightly out of place. This was definitely one.

I looked at my watch but it was still not working. I could see the moisture inside the crystal. I was going to ask what time it was, but decided to let it go. After all, there was no place I needed to be.

"Let's see," I said, thinking about where I had left off, "I had been flipping houses for about two years and had done fairly well at the beginning, but my heart wasn't in it. I was still unhappy and I had spent the last six months mostly trying to achieve happiness or more happiness. Whatever way you want to look at it is fine with me. I know that we've gone over this several times already. But that's the way it was. I stopped flipping houses and spent all my time trying to find a solution to my everlasting problem. But I was running out of money, and finally gave up temporarily and decided to get a job. It didn't take long to find a good paying job. A few days later I also ran across a good deal on another house, which I bought and moved into. I had decided that I might as well just live the way everyone else does, which means working at a job, paying the bills, and saving a little for old age. My son was living with me and I thought I'd better set a good example. The thought of going through life like this, waiting for the end to come, was terribly depressing but that's all I could see."

"About five month into the job, I walked in one morning and was told I was laid off. They told me that it was because business was slow and they needed to cut back. But that wasn't the real reason. They saw that I was unhappy. I just couldn't hide it anymore. I didn't have the energy to constantly put a smile on my face. I'm sure that they came to the conclusion that I was not happy working there."

"The whole thing came as a shock. I wasn't really upset, but at the same time, neither did I know what to do next. I sat around the house for a week, not doing much more than taking my dog for his daily walks. I had a little bit of money but not much, and the house payments were fairly high. It wasn't a big house but it was in a good area. The economy was fairly slow and there weren't many good paying jobs out there. Even if I managed to get a mediocre job right away, I knew I still wouldn't be able to hang onto the house. I remember sitting at the park and watching Rudy, my dog, run around and play with the other dogs, and something clicked. For some reason I decided that maybe I should give finding happiness one more try. I thought that maybe in all the books that I had read in the past that perhaps I missed something or not followed the instructions correctly. As soon as Rudy and I came home from our walk at the park, I jumped into the car and headed for the library. On the way to the library part of me was thinking that this was a total waste of time, yet another part of me had sprung to life with the greatest enthusiasm. I also realized that whenever I was throwing myself into the work of discovering inner happiness I actually became happy. It's after a while of not being able to go beyond that temporary happiness that I would get really depressed. I had a very strong feeling that this time I would succeed. I remember thinking that all I need to do is find that something that I had missed. Then everything would be fine."

"Gee whiz, how long does this go on for?" Danny interrupted me.

"This is it," I answered. "This is where it all began to change."

"Thank God, this was starting to depress me! Are we getting close to the lottery part?"

"Just about there."

"Anyway, I picked up a whole bunch of books on everything I could think of about meditation, spiritualism, visualization, mind control, positive thinking, Love, and so on, even a couple books on dowsing which didn't really fit. But I saw them and decided to take them with me. I spent several weeks reading, making notes, and following any instructions as best as I could. I read from the time that I got up in the morning until I went to bed. The only breaks I took were either to have something to eat or take Rudy to the park and to practice whatever was suggested in the various books."

"Did you achieve any results?" she asked.

"Not really," I answered. "Other than making the effort, which did make me feel good, or at least better than usual. I didn't actually expect any results. It was just a drive to try again that was bubbling in me. Making the effort gave me a sense of hope, and in many ways that was very comforting. Actually there's a difference between hoping to get something and expecting it to happen. But we'll talk more about that later."

"So this is where everything began to change. I was getting quite restless and decided I needed a break. I decided to phone a friend of mine to see if he was at home. I picked up some beer and headed over to see him."

"At that time, my friend was not financially in any better shape than I was. He wasn't working and didn't have much money. He spent most of his time watching sports and playing the sports lottery. He wasn't doing very well with the sports lottery. I was looking at some of his losing tickets. Sarcastically, I suggested that he might as well use a dart to pick which team is going to win. He laughed, and told me that I was probably right. I've always considered gambling like throwing money into the wind and hoping that twice as much will blow back at you. There's not much chance of that happening. I had played some bullshit poker in the past, but mostly for fun. The most you could win or lose was five or ten dollars."

"Looking over my friend's tickets, a thought occurred to me. I had just read several books on dowsing and had watched a program about it on TV. This particular fellow was dowsing for minerals and on this particular program he was working for a miner to help him find some pockets of certain minerals in an old abandoned mine. As it turned out they were quite successful. The dowser was using a simple piece of string, with some kind of weight at the other end. It looked like he was using a left spin for yes and a right spin for no. I thought that the bottom line is that the string is probably nothing more than a way for the subconscious mind to communicate with the conscious my mind."

"I looked at my friend and suggested that maybe a person could use their subconscious mind to see into the future and figure out who was going to win the game. He thought I was nuts and said that there was no way to predict the future, and he gave me about 20 reasons why it would not work. It's pretty obvious to me that he is a lot more thick-headed then I am."

"But the more I thought about it, the more I liked the idea. By the time I got home, I had it more or less worked out it in my mind. I figured all I needed to do was to find a state of mind where the conscious and subconscious come together and work together as one rather than being separate. It sounds simple, even though it took me some time to work it all out. It did turn out to be very simple, except that I was going to get more than I bargained for."

"What is so important about the subconscious?" Danny asked.

"The subconscious seems to have an enormous amount of information available to it. I also believe that all subconscious minds are connected like a giant network, but most importantly, I believe that the subconscious is also connected to our soul…that larger part of ourselves."

"It took me a while to work out the details and figure out a plan. I went back to the library and picked up a few more books. I played around with it for about a week or two, trying different things out. Anyway I took all the information I could find and mixed it all up, a little bit from here and a little bit from there. The conclusion that I came to was that I needed to be in a very deep meditating state, or a trance-like state of mind. There seemed to be a veil between the conscious mind and the subconscious mind that I was trying to pass through. The biggest problem was what to focus on. At first I tried to focus on the game results, but that just caused me to fall into a dream like state, and the results that I saw in my mind were not correct. Then I tried to focus on my subconscious and with that I had some mixed results, but not what I wanted."

"I'm going to spare you the details of all the stuff I went through to come to the conclusion that I came to. The bottom line is, we are much more than just conscious mind and unconscious mind. I came to the conclusion that I need to be in touch with the total part of whatever I am. And rather than saying 'all that I am' or 'higher self,' I decided to use the word soul to describe my total self."

"I was positive that connecting to that larger part of myself was the key, and it worked. Actually it worked so well that within six weeks I had won over one hundred and thirty times."

"How much money are we talking about?" Danny interrupted.

I took a sip from my drink. Looking at Danny, it wasn't hard to see the dollar signs in his eyes.

"The total amount of money was just under two thousand dollars, because I was making small bets. I wasn't going to take what little money I had and throw it into the wind. Also I figured that it was best to keep a low profile, and as long as it works, I might just as well take it slow. At that point the money seemed secondary. I felt I had accomplished something that the entire world would say is impossible. I literally felt like I was walking on air."

"What about happiness?" Neena asked.

"I guess it went on the back burner for a while," I answered. "It's allot easier being unhappy if you're doing it in a warm place under a palm tree watching the surf come in. I wasn't there yet but it was a definite possibility. Looking back now, I was happy. I was putting in allot of hours, but at the same time I enjoyed it immensely. Even today I still spend countless hours discovering things that I can do with my mind. I guess you could say I found my calling. But even though I still enjoy it today, and it makes me happy, it's not where my happiness comes from, nor was it the reason for my unhappiness. But we'll get to that shortly."

"Well, if you're going to be depressed, you might as well be comfortable," Danny observed.

"Something was definitely happening. Happiness was starting to bubble up from inside. And it did have something to do with the way I was using my mind. But at that time, the only thing I really noticed was that I seemed really at peace."

"That makes sense," said Neena. "You need inner peace to create happiness!"

"I agree," I said. "I was busy and excited, and temporarily really didn't care about anything else. But you also…"

"Never mind that!" Danny interrupted. "I need the exact instructions."

I hadn't noticed it before, but Danny already had a pen in his hand and a note pad opened in front of him. His eyes where as big as dandelions, and his lip was quivering more than ever.

"It's probably better if I tell you the rest of the story first."

"I would rather hear the rest of it," Neena said.

"I'd rather have the instructions now, otherwise you'll probably forget." Danny interjected.

"Well, I might forget," I laughed. "But I'm sure that you won't forget to remind me."

Neena shrugged her shoulders. "It's your choice."

This just seemed too strange. I wasn't sure whether Danny was just playing a game or if he was serious. You see there are actually two types of players. One plays with the universe and one is just in the game. The main difference is that the one that plays with the universe is really close to the dealer and generally knows what direction the game is supposed to go, and will work in that direction. They also know who has what cards. The rest, like myself, just play along with the game. I was sure that Neena and Danny were playing the game with the universe but now it appeared that perhaps only Neena was. So perhaps Danny was playing along with the game like me. Sometimes the universe seems to make the game up as it goes along, or at least that's how it appears to me.

This was not the first time that I have had to struggle with making this decision about whether to put the instructions into the book or even tell anyone about it. It appears that once again I'm at the crossroads. It just didn't seem to make any sense to me that the universe was leaving an important decision like this up to me. Or was it?

I decided to give Danny his instructions but first I thought it might be a good idea to give him a little lecture. To be honest it was more to make sure that I covered my own butt.

"OK, I'll give you the instructions, but I want you to know that this can be used for a lot of different things and if you decide to use it for gambling, then you take the responsibility of whatever happens onto your own shoulders. If you're going to spend two dollars on a ticket anyway, that's fine you might as well give yourself the best odds you can. But if you're going to throw your grocery money into this, I can tell you right now that you are going to lose, and I'll explain the reason for that to you..."

"I agree, no problem," he said, like a child with a new toy.

I took a sip from my orange juice and thought to myself, I've definitely heard those words spoken before.

Dreams

Dreams, oh sweet dreams
They say
If it is dreamable
Then it is also achievable.
I see that now, ever so clearly....
The question is,
Will I remember?
When I wake up?

Chapter Eight

"The first thing you need to understand is the need factor. It's like this: if you walk into a poker game with your last twenty dollars and you need to win, you might as well just throw your money on the table and leave, because if you need something really bad, it's going to be hard to get. The best way to describe it is to say that you need to be detached from the results."

Danny put down his pad and gave me a puzzled look. "You seemed to need the money pretty badly at that time. How is that different?"

"Actually, in many ways at that time I was at a point in my life where I really didn't care. If I won, fine, and if I didn't, so what? I also knew about the need factor. That's something I had learned the hard way many years before. There's a really big difference between wanting something or needing something. The difference is very simple: when we really want something, we tend to think about it and work out ways how to get it. But when we get to the point where we feel we desperately need it, our minds are not going to be clear. Instead we'll be thinking about what will happen if we don't succeed. It's like trying to look in one direction and walk or drive in another direction. It doesn't work. The mind works the same way. The mind needs to be focused on what we want to achieve and not what we are afraid might happen if we don't succeed."

"So, it's like I have to do it just for fun or for something to do, like a hobby." Danny said.

"That's a perfect way to start. That way you're not under any pressure and you can focus just on what you want to achieve. If you put a lot of money into it, then you are going to be attached to the results, but if you only throw in two or three dollars it really doesn't matter, especially if you were going to do that anyway."

"Are you sure you understand what Klaus is saying, Danny?" Neena asked quietly.

"I get it, no problem," he answered. "What's next?"

"Next you need a quiet place, a place where you won't get disturbed. You need to either lie down or sit in a comfortable chair. I prefer lying down because that way I don't have to worry about my head drooping over. The only problem with lying down is that it may take a little more work to stay awake. Then you need to let yourself relax totally and let your body go to sleep, but not your mind. Just lie there and allow your body to fall asleep to the point where you can't feel your body anymore nor hear anything. Turning off your hearing is not totally necessary, but it definitely helps and can make quite a difference in the end."

"Should I visualize something so that my brain stays awake?"

"No! Because if you start visualizing, you'll fall into a dream-like state and from there you'll fall asleep. And if you visualize at that point, then chances are the things you see will be imaginary."

"So what do I do with my mind to stay awake?"

"That's the tricky part. You need to focus on your soul. I define your soul as that larger part of yourself or the total of what you are, whatever that may be for you. The problem is that you cannot visualize it. The best way I have found so far to do this is to pretend that I am listening to my soul. I pretend that I am trying to hear something that is far away and very faint. Just take a moment and pretend that you are trying to hear what is going on outside this bar."

Danny closed his eyes and was totally still. I noticed that he was holding his breath.

"No, don't hold your breath. Do everything that you're doing with your mind, but keep breathing."

Danny opened his eyes. "I think I get it. My mind was totally focused, but it wasn't doing anything at all. Actually it was totally blank."

"That's right, but the hardest part is to maintain that focus without thinking any other thoughts. It's not hard to do it for a few seconds, but after that the mind tries to bring up images and thoughts. No matter what happens, you can't engage those thoughts. If you find yourself doing that or involving yourself with the images in your mind you have to bring your mind back to focusing on your soul. If you don't catch yourself drifting, then you will enter a dream state and from there most likely fall asleep. Another very important thing is to focus, but do it in a relaxed state. You can't strain otherwise you won't be relaxed and you'll end up with a headache. So you need to be relaxed mentally, physically, and emotionally, but focused at the same time. It sounds difficult but in fact it's quite natural."

"Why can't you just visualize the results in your mind?" Neena asked.

"I was just going to ask that too!" Danny said.

"I don't know exactly why. All I know is that if you start visualizing at that early stage, then somehow what you see will be from the Dream State, and will not be correct. I don't have all the answers but I believe that you need to pass the Dream State by in order to reach that higher part of your mind. It's almost like a gateway on a path; you can turn left or right, with left being the Dream State and right being the higher mind. At first it will be difficult to keep yourself from turning left. We do that naturally, but only because we have done it so many times and for most people the path to the higher mind or soul has not been used very much. It's like following a groove; it has a tendency to pull you towards the left."

"That makes sense. I think I understand. But what makes you think that my soul will help me?" Danny asked dubiously.

"That's a good question, but I never looked at it like that. I believe I am reaching and becoming the larger part of myself, and with attaining that state, having all the resources available to me. Why would you use an old hand-held calculator when you have a very large and fast computer in your closet? If you have to make important life decisions why use that small conscious mind when you have this incredible resource available?"

"Think about it this way. Whenever you are trying to make decisions you are in a sense trying to predict the future, even if you're making a simple decision like what time to cook supper. When will everyone be there? What time? How long will it take? And so on. The conscious mind is only capable of making very small and slow calculations but the larger part of you, your subconscious, has more information available to it, and carries all the memories of everything that you have seen, heard, smelled, felt, or experienced in its memory. So it can use that information to calculate things out much more quickly and more accurately than the conscious mind. To give you an example, the subconscious mind has a photographic memory. Everything that is seen by your eyes…even if you do not consciously see it…is recorded in the subconscious, and the most remarkable part is that all subconscious minds are somehow connected. It's like a computer that is connected to thousands of other computers and can download any information that it needs from anywhere. Scientists are still debating this today but that is knowledge that has been around for thousands of years. Then comes the higher mind or the part that I call my soul, and this part of me lives beyond time and physical restrictions."

I stopped for a moment to give Danny a chance to ask his question because he was squirming around like a child who needed to go to the bathroom. "Why would you focus on your soul when you say that the subconscious has so much information available to it?"

"I don't have all the answers, but over the years I have read many books and I like to read in between the lines. Nobody has came right out and said that they have tried this, but I believe that many have, and many have tried to use visualization and have failed. I also believe that many have tried to use the subconscious and failed. To be honest I can only guess at the reasons why those two ways don't work, but if I spent all my time trying to figure out the reasons I would never get anywhere. I believe that we are more than just conscious mind and subconscious mind. I believe that very few, if any, have tried using their soul."

"Why do you think that?" Neena asked.

"I have more theories than answers. But a lot might have to do with superstition and fear. I think that it mostly has to do with fear because my friend was afraid to try it, even though he is not religious in any way, because he thought I might be breaking some cosmic law. It appears that this has been a very well kept secret and has only been passed down to a few masters.

"Why do you think that they kept it a secret?" she asked.

"Actually that's a good question. I'm a little bit concerned myself," he said.

"Probably because of fear," I answered.

"What would these masters be afraid of?" she asked.

Danny nodded his head as if to say he was asking the same question.

"Probably darkness. Having knowledge does not always take away fear and having knowledge does not necessarily make you strong enough to face whatever life may throw at you."

"You don't seem to have that much knowledge, so why are you not afraid to play with something that has been hidden for centuries?" asked Danny.

I laughed at his question. "What's the universe going to threaten me with? I've already tried to end my life several times. The only thing that remains is immortality, which would just give me more time to get into more trouble. I now have something that is a thousand times more powerful than anything that is dark and negative. Why would a larger part of you be upset for connecting with it? That was not what they were trying to hide. It was what you are capable of doing and achieving when you connect to that larger part of yourself. I have something much more fascinating than this lottery stuff."

"What's that?" Danny put down his pen. His lip was definitely quivering now.

I smiled to myself. "I told you to listen to the rest of the story first, but you insisted. So you'll have to wait until I finish giving you the instructions. But first I need my orange juice refreshed and I'm going to the washroom. Then I'll give you the rest of the instructions you so desperately wanted."

I was still smiling to myself on the way to the washroom. I was thinking of something that my friend John used to tell me. "Always keep an ace in your sleeve. You may never use it, but even if you have nothing, you'll feel like you have something…"

Fear

The fears of trying
Will, in the end,
Shed the tears
Of Love
"I sure hope I am right about this one…"

Chapter Nine

The bathroom was very extremely tiny. It had one sink and one stall with a small door on it. I entered the stall and closed the door behind me. I was thinking that maybe I should not have mentioned the lottery information. Maybe I should have kept it a secret. But on the other hand there are so many beneficial things that can be done with it. I heard the bathroom door open and I thought I heard some footsteps. As the door closed I heard what sounded like an older man's voice.

He said, "Do not be afraid to tell what you know. Just leave the rest to me."

"Oh yeah, and who are you?" I answered sarcastically; thinking perhaps Danny was playing a joke on me. I opened the stall door expecting to see Danny standing there, but no one was there. I quickly exited the bathroom and scanned the bar, but there was no one but Danny, Neena, and the old man sitting at the table. I thought that there is no way that old man could have gotten back to his table that quickly, and he looked like he hadn't even moved. Danny and Neena were staring at me wondering why I was standing there. I walked back to my stool and sat down.

"Did anybody come into the bathroom while I was in there?" They both looked at me and at each other, and shook their heads.

"I don't suppose that stuff in the green bottle makes you hallucinate, by any chance?" I asked.

"Not me," Danny shook his head. "How about you, Neena?"

"I'm fine." She shrugged her shoulders.

"It's probably the Scotch. That stuff is usually good for a couple of pink elephants. What did you see?" Danny asked.

"I thought I heard something, but it doesn't matter. Let's get back to the instructions."

"Good idea." Danny picked up his pen.

"Now as you are doing this exercise, you may come to a point where you begin to hear things, like words or music, or even just sounds. Also you may come to a point where pictures will form in your mind, but you don't need to be concerned about this. The best thing to do is just let it happen without involving yourself. These things are just echoes in your mind. By the way, this is also a very good sign because you are very close to where you want to be."

I sipped my orange juice to give Danny a chance to catch up with his notes.

"So what are these visions and sounds that you will hear?" she asked.

"My theory is that the mind, especially the subconscious mind, never stops. I believe that at this point you are contacting the subconscious mind, but the important part is to keep going, allowing yourself to drift even deeper, and just keep focusing on your soul, no matter what you see or hear."

Danny looked up from his notes. "How do I know when I have reached my soul?"

"That's a good question. Actually it's achieved in degrees. It's something that becomes more each time you do it. But you'll know when you're there. Some of the signs are that you will feel very peaceful, and you may have a sense of being larger. Your mind will also be very clear. It's hard to explain, but once you're there, there is nothing like it. You might also feel that you are more connected to the universe and at the same time separated from everyday concerns. That's the only way I can describe it. I believe that it is a little different for everyone."

I stopped for a moment to give Danny another chance to catch up with his notes. Apparently he was writing down every single word.

"How is Danny going to know what the results of the games are?"

"That's the fun part. At this point you have some choices to make because you can do a lot of different and fascinating things that I will tell you about later, but if you choose to go the route of trying to figure out the game results then so be it. Now, everything that I have told you so far you need to follow exactly. This path is very narrow and you need to stay focused."

"I'm ready!" he smiled.

"OK. At this point you can begin to visualize. What I like to do is pretend that I'm moving forward in time and place myself at the corner grocery store. Then I imagine that I'm walking in the store towards the lottery counter and I look directly at the game result sheets. Originally, I pretended that I was on a train and each town we passed represented one day in the future. When I got to the day I wanted to be at, the train would stop, I would get off and walk to a newspaper stand and look at the results in the daily newspaper. But I found that sometimes I was using too much of my imagination. Later I realized that was because I was trying to make the train too real, rather than just having the sensation of being in a train."

"How do I know whether I'm just imagining what I see?" he asked.

"Some of it will be your imagination; there's no way to get around that. The best way I've found is to imagine the store or the train, whichever you choose, and imagine them very lightly, so that it does not become your reality but just a form to measure time with. But when you look at the results, you need to visualize very clearly, but use your imagination as little as possible. You should not do it for too long a time period. I have also had very good success by simply asking my soul to put the answers into my mind. In such a way that I would see it as if I was looking at a screen with the answers projected onto the screen. It's just a matter of trying different things and discovering what works best for you. If the answers are incorrect then it is not that your soul is giving you the wrong answers, it's that you not receiving the information correctly."

"How long did it take you to achieve this?" she asked.

"About ten days."

"That's not bad," he said.

"You need to remember that at that time I was not working and I was mostly spending my entire day working on this. There are also some minor things that you need to know. Not every answer that you receive will be correct, for various reasons. The future is not carved in stone and it can change at any time. So I tried to get the information from six to ten different games. Then later I would look at those answers and compare them to what I would have done. Then I would select two or three games and play them. Sometimes if I felt I was having a good day and the information was very clear, I would play more games, but only when if it felt right. I also made very small bets and I made combinations. Let's say I had ten games. I might play three or four sets with three or four games in each set. That way if there was a mistake, the winnings would still out number the losses."

"It seems so simple, yet I can see that there is a little bit of work involved. So is that all there is to it?" he asked.

"That's it!" I answered. "Well maybe just one more thing. Be aware of what appears to be beginners luck!"

"What does that mean?"

"You'll see."

"Hey, that's not..."

"I see it!" said Neena, sitting up straight on her stool. "Oh, God, that's...Wow, I almost missed it! Don't you see it, Danny?"

"Hold on! If someone can't see it, they're not ready. It's never to be spoken."

She put her hand across her mouth and smiled. "Mum's the word."

"That's not funny." Danny jumped off his stool and picked up his notes.

I was smiling so much I could almost feel my lips touching my ears.

He looked up from his notes at me. "Who do you think you are? The dealer?"

Trying to control the grin on my face, I thought to myself, 'I'm not the dealer, but I know when I'm holding more than one card.' When you play with the universe in the right way, which is with respect, Love, and kindness, the universe keeps giving you more cards. I have heard it said that when you receive a full deck then the universe might let you deal a few cards. That's more responsibility than I'm interested in and I imagine to get so many cards a person would have to be very dedicated to making a difference in this world. I suppose someone like Mother Teresa would perhaps have had a few decks. It's hard to say; all I know for sure is that three or four cards can get you a long way.

Inner Child

Ever notice
That in every
Adult body
There is a child
Kicking to get
Out?
Maybe we should let them out
Before they wreck the place.

Chapter Ten

Danny was totally beside himself about the little secret Neena and I were keeping. I told him that there would be quite a few clues in the rest of the story. That seemed to settle him for the moment. It's not really a secret, it's one of those things that if you try to put into words, it will be molded in a person's mind, and the minute it is formed into a mold it's no longer what it was. Some things in the universe cannot be put into words. Doing so destroys it for that moment and in a sense you would end up giving someone something that was totally useless. The biggest problem is that if you try to tell someone, then they will mold it and later when they come to see this information in its true form, then again they will automatically put it in a mold, and so the information is lost.

I looked at Danny. "Before I continue with the rest of the story, I should probably tell you something that I just realized I had forgotten to mention."

"That's a surprise," Danny smiled sarcastically.

"This is actually very important, especially if you're having trouble keeping your mind focused on your soul. I've read a lot of books on Eastern meditation over the years and many of them mention various areas of the mind that you can meditate on, but none of them ever mention the brain stem. It's sort of like this. I don't like to go into a dark basement even if there is a light on because there are so many dark areas where the basement monsters can hide. I have found that the best way to deal with dark basement is to put a light in the darkest area. The brain works in much the same way."

For some reason Neena thought this was very amusing.

"When you are trying to focus on your soul, in a sense you are using what some Yogis call the higher mind. But part of your mind will try to bring up other thoughts. That's something I constantly struggled with. The question was, which part of the mind was doing this? So I took a look at all the parts of the mind that the meditation books mention. I always like to look for strange things, things that don't really fit, but appear quite normal, or too normal."

"What do you mean?" she asked curiously.

"Take a look at eastern writings from yogis or masters. If you ask them a question they will give you a very short answer, yet if you give them a pen and some paper they will write until the cows come home. Rather inconsistent, don't you think?"

"Do you think that means something?" Danny asked.

I nodded my head. "If it's there, it means something. How about the fact that even though they are from different races and different countries, they all have the same writing patterns? I use to ponder over the fact that they wrote hundreds and hundreds of pages and say next to nothing. Not only that they also write everything over and over and everything is the same, only the angle and approach is different. Let's face it, they must be writing in some form of code, and if they all know what this code is, then it can't be that hard to decipher. When someone can write ten books and say nothing that's fascinating because then they must be writing between the lines. So I look in places they tell you not to bother looking, and I dig in places that they never mention…"

"After all, if you have a treasure and you want to tell someone about it, but not let them know where it is, or exactly how to get it unless they're willing to follow you, then you will have to spin quite the web."

"So the problem I found is that you can't reach your soul or that larger part of yourself unless you turn off your mind from gibbering like a chicken that has just laid an egg, and the key to that is the one thing they seem to omit. Turn it off, and you're in."

For a minute I was proud of myself, then I realized that I was like a rooster on a fence post, clucking and bragging to the chicken next to him. Boy I hate it when that happens.

"You must be really proud of yourself, figuring all that out," she said, gently pushing the thorn deeper.

"I've tried meditation before and have had problems with thoughts creeping in. How do I turn them off?" he asked.

"That's a piece of cake. First you get yourself all relaxed and calm, then just for a minute visualize that there is a beam of light coming from your soul and going right down from the top of your head, filling the whole area with very bright light. Don't keep on visualizing this, just keep it in the back of your mind. It's like if a carpenter was on your roof repairing it, you don't need to stand there and watch him all day, you just know that he is there. So in not so many words, you just leave the light there without constantly focusing on it. That will keep the whole area very busy. I don't know exactly what this area of the brain is supposed to do, but I know this works and that's all that really matters at this point."

"Danny, tell Klaus about the basement monsters." Neena changed the subject.

He shook his head. He had a look of fear on his face.

Neena leaned towards me. "We have a basement here, but Danny won't go there because he thinks there are a monsters down there. Would you like to take a look?"

"I don't think so…If Danny says there are monsters in the basement, then that's good enough for me."

She laughed. "You men are all alike! You make a lot of noise, but when the wolf comes, you're no where to be found."

I decided to let that comment go, and thought about where I had left off before I got sidetracked.

Secrets of the Universe

The key
Thought, Trust

The lock
Action, Love

The door
Result, Joy

The game
Continuance.

Not!

Chapter Eleven

"During those six weeks, weird things had started to happen. I couldn't explain them so I just assumed that my awareness had increased and I was becoming more sensitive to what was going on around me. I didn't really want to face some of the things that were going on, so I thought that the best thing to do was just to ignore them. Things started slowly. First I felt like I was being watched. You know the feeling; it's like someone is staring at you. Mostly I felt it at night, so I started leaving the lights on. The next thing that started happening was also in the evenings. I would be sitting in the living room with my dog Rudy, and sometimes he would suddenly sit up, point his ears forward, and stare at the center of the room as if he was looking at something. He did this many times over the weeks. I could never see or hear anything, but sometimes I definitely felt like something was staring at me. The most interesting part was that if Rudy decided to leave the living room, he would go around the area that he was staring at, even though going straight across is what he would have done normally."

"The next thing that started happening was things moving around. For instance, I would put something down somewhere, perhaps a cup or a book, and later it would be somewhere else. I tried to tell myself that I must not have been paying attention to what I was doing, but somewhere in the back of my mind, I knew that was not the problem. I live very simply and with very few things, but the things I do have are always in their

place. One afternoon I laid down to go into my meditation to select my
bets, but I had forgotten to turn up the heat. When I go into a very deep
meditation my body temperature tends to drop quite a bit. I had already
begun relaxing when I could felt myself becoming cold. I didn't want to
get up and have to start all over again. Then I heard the furnace go on and
thought maybe I had turned up the thermostat, and continued with my
meditation. By the time I was finished, the house was extremely hot. After
getting up I went to the thermostat to turn it down, but looking at it, I
realized I had never turned it up. It was set at just under 70 degrees but the
room temperature had reached 80 degrees and while I was looking at the
thermostat, I heard the furnace turn off.

"Over those six weeks, I also had several strange dreams. In two of them
I recalled talking to an angel but I could never totally remember the dream
or what was said. I also had several dreams where I was sword fighting but
I couldn't remember any details. Normally if these types of things were
happening it would have fascinated me, but I wanted to stay focused on
getting the correct sports results."

"Now this is where things began to take on a new twist," I said.
"Towards the last week I was having trouble seeing the results. I could see
the page but I was having trouble seeing the actual scores. It was almost
like someone was putting their thumb over the answers. As I moved my
perception from one area on the score sheet to another there was a dark
area that followed. I was still having success but it was taking an enormous
amount of time and concentration. I thought that perhaps it was just my
own doubts interfering, which is not an uncommon thing. Each day it
became more and more difficult and each day I put more and more effort
into it. There was no way that I was going to let a little problem like that
ruin my achievement. I thought that perhaps over the weeks I had gotten
lazy and was not going deep enough into my meditation. So every time I
started meditating, I made a great effort to go deeper. During this time I
purchased some earmuffs…the kind that construction workers use when
they work with noisy machinery. The earmuffs made a big difference in

my ability to concentrate. I had also purchased a sleep mask to put over my eyes. With the sleep mask and the earmuffs I was able to go much deeper without being disturbed. I still use them today, because if someone slams a door or drops something I'm not shocked out of whatever mind state I may be in."

"November 6," I stopped to take a drag from my cigarette. "That was the day when the shit hit the fan."

"I'm not blind. I saw it coming, but I just didn't expect this."

I could see on Danny's face that this was making him nervous.

"You know what, I just remembered something I forgot to tell you! It's a big piece of the puzzle. I think it's one of the main keys."

"Are you nuts?" Danny asked. "You're going to leave us hanging in suspense?"

She laughed. "Just give him another shot of the good stuff. That will keep his lips moving."

"Just give me another minute, this is truly important." I said, knowing full well that Danny was irritated, probably because he thought this had something to do with the lottery, and he probably thought this meant he would not be able to give it a try.

He stepped off his stool and grabbed a glass, threw some ice in it, grabbed the bottle, and poured a full glass.

She laughed.

He put the glass in front of me and put the open bottle next to it.

"There! Now let's see those lips move!" He sat down again on his stool.

I thought to myself, 'I don't know what game the universe is playing now, but I'll figure it out before the night is over.' I looked over my shoulder to see if the old man was still sitting at the table. He was. He had not even moved an inch, nor had anyone tried to serve him. That's very strange. I debated saying something, but decided maybe it would be best if I just left it alone and see what happened.

I turned towards Neena. "About three weeks after first having success in winning the sports lottery, I figured that it might be a good idea if I tried to travel into the future to see what my future self is doing. I thought that if I can travel into the future to see the sports results then I should also be able to travel in the future to see how my life is turning out. It took three or four tries, I can't exactly remember, but nevertheless I did succeed."

"I found that while I'm trying to see into the future, the picture in my mind can take a bit of time to form completely. At first what I saw appeared to be myself sitting on a lawn chair in front of a fire pit. Next some grass and trees and various other things formed. At first I thought he was sitting perhaps in the woods. But then a cabin or a summerhouse appeared 20 to 30 feet behind him. I was looking directly at my future self when I noticed he was staring at me, and at the same time I saw that there was an angel sitting in another lawn chair beside him. I tried to clear my vision by removing anything that was possibly caused by imagination. At the same time I was trying to clear my perception, my future self pointed at me, looked towards the angel, then back towards me and said, "I can't believe it he finally made it!" They both started to laugh loudly.

"For some reason I couldn't hold myself there and was instantly pulled back to my normal awake state. I sat up in my bed and thought about it for a while, and decided that maybe I had imagined the whole thing or at least part of it. I decided to try again some other time, but I never got the chance."

The Joker Card

I call it the Joker card even though it is no joke. It's the reason I never wanted to play the game. I figured out the game when I was still fairly young and about the same time I realized I was holding one of these cards. This can be a real problem, especially if you don't understand it. I have seen a lot of people carry this card and have seen the problems it can cause. One of the biggest issues with this card is that you do not have a choice. If the universe gives you one, then that's it. There's no throwing it down. You can't run and you can't hide, and there's no way to fight it. I believe that there is a choice but it's made by our higher self, and once that decision is made, it's done. This card can mean different things for different people but generally, this card plays you. You do not play it. You're probably asking what does this card do? If you have one of these cards, one way or another you are going to be directed to do something in this life that will make a difference. Unfortunately I can't narrow that down for you.

Many years ago I went to a very gifted person for help. I asked her, "What is the matter with my life? I try to go a certain direction and it seems like the universe tries to slam me into a different direction. How do I fight this?" She said "You are holding a card, and you know it, but you have chosen to fight it, and you will lose! There is nothing I can do for you." I was furious, and responded, "I will fight to the end. I will stand and I will win." As I walked out I heard her say; "You will lose."

You're probably asking why anyone would want to fight this card. To be quite honest, there are very few people who have this card and do not fight it.

Why? Because this card will lead you down what appears to be totally illogical paths, and you will be pushed in directions that will make absolutely no sense. This card is not a map; all you see is one step. It will push your faith to the absolute limit, and beyond. Why? It would take too long for me to explain, nor am I sure my theory is correct. I can give you a clue: After you have finished reading this book, look at how everything has unfolded and you will see very easily that this book is my card, and the game is not over.

How do you know if you have one of these cards? Here are several clues.

First: You may feel that in some way you should be doing something more useful with your life or that there is something more important for you than just living day to day, but you have no idea what that something is.

Second: You may have a sense of urgency to do something, but may have no clue about what to do.

Third: Somehow you are being pushed in certain directions and if you try to go in a different direction, it seems like all hell breaks loose.

Fourth: You might feel that you are constantly searching for or craving something, but are not sure what it is.

Now just take a moment and become very quiet. Think. Are you holding one of these cards?

Spare yourself the agony of trying to fight it.

Been there, done that, didn't like it.

PS: This card can also be time delayed. In other words, it's there, but hasn't fully kicked in yet, but the effects are still felt by the person holding the card.

The Dealer

The players
The writers
The readers
Are all in the game.

Chapter Twelve

"Before I tell you the rest," I said, "You need to understand that on November 6, my whole life got turned upside down. Although I remember virtually everything, some things may not be exactly in the order that they happened."

"Is he stalling, or am I mistaken? "Danny asked Neena.

"Oh, he's stalling, big time," she said.

"No, not really," I answered. "I'm just trying to cover all the bases. I don't want there to be any misunderstandings."

They sat there quietly, staring at me. It almost looked like they were trying to make me feel guilty. Like that's going to work? A strange shiver went up my spine and out of the top of my head. I got the strange impression that maybe I was pushing my luck.

"Usually I go to the store fairly early in the morning to get the results and the list of who is going to play that day. But I had slept in after a very restless night. Also for some reason I really didn't feel like doing it that day. Something just didn't sit right with me. After lunch I took Rudy out for his walk and on the way back from the park we stopped at the store and picked up the sports information. I still had lots of time because the bets usually do not need to be in before 5 or 6 p.m. Going into a deep meditation right after taking a long walk seems to work really well. So as soon as we got home, I went into the bedroom to lie down. I keep the list of games in one hand so that I could study it just before I close my eyes. I keep a pen and note pad at my right side so that I can write down the results without having to get up. I had my sleep mask and ear muffs on, so there was little chance of me being disturbed. So there I was, lying on my bed slowly relaxing, and going deeper. Because of the difficulty that I had been having over the previous two weeks, this whole process took at least two hours. I was just getting to the point where my body was starting to become numb when I heard what sounded like someone clearing his throat. Thinking it was Rudy. I continued, and a few minutes later there was a thud under my bed. Loud noises like this will usually bring me back to my normal awake state, which means I need to start all over again. This time I thought that maybe it was just a wooden support holding up the mattress. Sometimes if I have trouble relaxing or getting started I will count backwards from a hundred to one and this usually allows me to relax at times when my mind does not want to. I started slowly counting backwards and after a few numbers I could swear that someone was counting with me. I could almost hear what seemed like a faint voice saying the numbers at exactly the same time I was. I stopped and listened, but I didn't hear anything. So I started counting again and within one or two numbers I could hear a very faint voice counting with me. I thought perhaps I was imagining things and I decided to skip the counting part and just lay here until my body went to sleep. I was just at the edge of where my body drifts off and at the point where all physical sensation and hearing disappear when something hit the bed hard enough to shake it. I thought a friend of mine had come over and had just shook the bed to wake me up. So I lifted my sleep mask and opened my eyes. But what I saw was not a friend of mine. In fact, I couldn't believe what I saw. My heart was pounding so hard that I thought it was going to rip a hole in my chest."

"I was face to face with an angel, a big angel, at least seven feet tall. He was brushing himself off, and said something like, "Hey! Don't you ever dust under there? We're talking major dust problems here, buddy." I still had my ear muffs on and couldn't hear a voice but I heard what he said in my head loud and clear."

I stopped for a moment to take another cigarette out of my package. Neena and Danny seemed like they were frozen in time. From the look on Danny's face I could see that he thought that the angel was going to rip a strip off of me. I lit my cigarette.

"That's not the type of language that I would expect to hear from an angel." I said. My body was frozen but my heart and my mind where going a billion miles an hour. I don't know how long we both stared at each other. He was smiling, but I don't think I was. Thoughts were racing around in my head. I thought this couldn't be real. Maybe he's here to give me shit, maybe because I'm not supposed to be using this yogi stuff to win the lottery. Maybe the universe has lost its patience with me. Maybe the universe has sent this angel to straighten me out. My whole body started to shake. I've been scared, but never that scared. I thought maybe I should jump out of the window, but I realized that wouldn't work. He was too close to the door for me to be able to walk past him. I could hear a part of me yelling. You have to get out of here, get out of here! Play along, I said to myself, that's it, just play along. I can talk my way out of this. Just say hi and play it cool."

"Somehow I managed to get one word out of my mouth. 'Hi.'"

"He leaned forward towards me. 'Well, what do you know? He speaks! Gee, relax. I think your eyeballs are going to pop right out of your head.'"

Just as I was starting to get comfortable with the situation, he yelled, "Boo!"

"Something in me just snapped."

Their faces were frozen.

"The angel smiled. 'There, now that you're breathing again, why don't we sit and have a nice chat?"

"That was it. I freaked out, jumped up, and launched for him. If I can't talk my way out, then I'll fight. I went right through him, into the wall, head first."

I stopped to take a sip of my Scotch and a few drags from my cigarette. Even now, just talking about it makes my heart pound.

Danny shook his head. "Are you nuts? You tried to jump an angel?"

Neena broke out in laughter, and Danny and I had no choice but to follow her lead.

One Tree Down

I remember a time when I was smaller, younger, faster, and my sword was swift.

One of my favorite games was sword fighting with the trees.

You might think that trees would not be very tough opponents, but they are. It's just a matter of picking on the right ones.

In every forest there are at least a half dozen or so that are into it. This is where it gets tricky. Some trees like to carry extremely flexible swords and you have to be careful how much force you use or they will snap back at you with twice the speed.

On the other hand, it is much less painful to be stabbed with a flexible sword than with the hard rigid ones. Those hard rigid ones will crack your sword in half right in the heat of the battle. Then you are stuck. The only thing you can do is run and hope some other tree will give you its sword. That is, if you're not already staggering around with one stuck in your back.

To this very day I can still remember my battle cries as I walk in the forest.

And I hear the call, "Come on, old man, we dare you!"

As my heart awakens and the adrenaline pumps, I move swiftly.

But there is only silence as I hug them, and surrender my Love.

Yes, many times I have been stabbed doing this; these scars I carry with pride and honor.

Challenge me, and I swear by my life:

I Will Squeeze the Very Love Out Of Your Pores.

In Love, to my friends, the Trees.

Chapter Thirteen

My Lucky Number

"I have never heard of anybody trying to pick a fight with an angel. If you thought you were in trouble, why would you make it worse?" Danny shook his head, still wiping the tears from his eyes.

I shrugged my shoulders. "I don't really know what got into me, other than being scared to death. I remember when he leaned forward and yelled 'Boo,' which I heard loud and clear even though I had my earmuffs on. I just snapped."

"So what happened next?" she asked.

"I hit the wall with my head, and that's all I remember. It must have knocked me out cold. When I came to, I was sitting hunched over on my chair in the living room. He was sitting on the sofa. As my focus came back I realized I could see right through him. When I reached for my forehead, I was surprised that there was no bump, not even a sore spot, and not even a headache. I felt like I just had a long nap. But there was a numbing calmness; my mind was quiet and my body was relaxed. There's no doubt in my mind that my head hit the wall because when your head hits something that hard there's a certain indescribable sound that you hear just before the lights go out. I remember looking at my watch. It was almost 6:30 PM. I was sure that it was only about 2:30 when I first laid down to work on my bets."

"I looked over at the angel and asked. 'Who are you?'"

"'It's pretty obvious, isn't it?'"

"I just stared at him. My mind was too numb to deal with it. The thought that I might be dreaming had occurred to me."

"'Let me give you a clue.' he grinned, and for some strange reason that grin looked familiar."

"'Wings. See?' he spread out his wings so I could get a better look. 'And look, feathers! And look, I glow and I can make the lights go on and off.'"

"I hadn't even noticed that the lights were on. I just sat there staring at him."

"'Wait! Don't guess yet. See there's a halo, and there's more. I can float; I can make myself really small and really big…Okay, I'll give you three guesses.'"

"My mind and my body was moving in slow motion. He just sat there while I tried to assemble my thoughts. He looked so familiar. Finally, I asked him why I felt like I knew him. As I asked that question. I realized that I was speaking in slow motion."

"'Whoa, you hit the nail right on the head! Or let's just say, in your case, you hit the wall on the head,' he laughed."

"The light came on in my head. For a second something came to my mind, even though it really didn't make sense."

"I pointed towards him. 'Sneaky.'"

"'Whoever said that banging your head against a wall serves no purpose obviously never met you. We're talking genius level here, my friend.'"

"There was no time for me to respond because instantly a gate in my mind opened. My head was spinning, and memories were flooding in like someone was downloading an entire lifetime. I barely made it to the washroom before throwing up. I don't know how long I was in there, but when I came out the angel was gone…which was probably a good thing because my head was on fire. Within a few minutes I was in my bed and out cold."

"Why would you have so many memories flooding into your mind to the point that it made you throw up?" Danny asked.

"That's a question that is still out for debate. Maybe by the end of the story you'll able to tell me."

"So who or what is Sneaky?" Neena asked.

"Sneaky is the angel's name. Let's just call him that for now, you'll see what happens towards the end of the story."

"If you never saw the angel before, how did you know what his name was?" Danny asked. "Besides, what kind of name is 'Sneaky?'"

They laughed. That's okay, I thought, because it's going to take every bit of their minds to put the pieces together and try to make sense out of it all, without driving themselves crazy.

"As far as the name is concerned, that will explain itself as I tell you the rest of the story. On the other hand, nothing is what it seems to be. And as far as your other question, there's no way for me to honestly answer that until I finish the whole story, providing that there really is an answer."

"There's always an answer," Danny said.

I shook my head. "You're free to believe that for as long as you like, but in this world nothing is as it appears, not even close."

"It seems pretty obvious to me you're either in over your head or you're in a lot of trouble," she observed.

"I'm putting my bets on both!" Danny laughed.

I took a drag from my cigarette. "We'll see. I may get scared sometimes, but that doesn't stop me. At least not for long."

For Sale

One Guardian Angel,
Twisted Sense of Humor,
As is, No warranty, No refund
Send check or money order to box...

Chapter Fourteen

Danny picked up his notebook and closed it. "I guess there's no point in saving these notes." He let out a deep sigh of disappointment.

"Why do you say that?"

"It's pretty obvious, isn't it?" he said. "Didn't this angel tell you that you couldn't do this?"

"No. And I'm not finished with the story."

"Then why did the angel come to see you?" Neena asked.

"Just hang in there, we'll get to that. Besides, who said he was an angel?"

"You said he was." Danny said.

"No I didn't. I said he *looked* like an angel. Remember what I said about things looking too perfect? I've never seen an angel. But if I do, I don't expect him to look like he just starred in a Hollywood movie."

Danny seemed a little relieved but also a little bit confused.

"If he wasn't an angel, then what was he?" Neena asked.

"I didn't say he *wasn't* an angel," I answered. "You know, if you want to understand the universe and its secrets, you can't be guessing, because that confuses the mind. You just take the facts and hang on to them like new pieces of a jigsaw puzzle and wait until other pieces fall into place. Figuring out the universe is more like a hunt than a guessing game. You hunt for the pieces, not guess about what they might be. Sometimes you need to take apart what you know to see the pieces individually, then put them back together to see the picture. That way you're not guessing but seeing a larger part of the truth one piece at a time."

"Okay then, how do we break apart everything that you have told us so far?" Neena asked.

"Let's take it apart," I answered "First, we have unhappiness, we have need, we have success, we have fear, failure, contemplation, future; we have what appears to be an angel, and so on. Now look at each piece."

I stopped and waited for them to think about what I said.

"The only picture I see is the one you told us about, no more," Danny said. "Without guessing, there's no more."

I looked at Neena but she shook her head.

"The problem is that you're not adding your master pieces," I said.

"What are master pieces?" asked Danny.

"Like everything in the universe is nothing more than a shadow of its opposite. Or an airplane isn't a plane without the sky. The truth is ever changing and expanding. That's why there's no such thing as the truth."

"I still don't get it," Danny shrugged his shoulders.

"Everything is but a shadow of its opposite. So take the piece we call unhappiness and break it in to its opposite. Now you have two pieces, unhappiness and…"

"Joy," she said, "and need is fulfillment. I see it now the whole picture has grown."

"I still don't get it." Danny sounded frustrated.

She looked towards me. "May I?"

"Please do." I was surprised that she had caught on so quickly.

"Danny, it's like this: all the pieces belong to a picture, but it's a picture with no end and no beginning. Everything just keeps connecting, but there are certain rules like if there is one piece, then somewhere its opposite will also exist. It might be bigger or smaller, that we don't know yet, but we know it's there, somewhere.

He looked bewildered as he tried to understand her.

"Let me explain it to you this way. A few minutes ago you said that for some reason you were not allowed to use these meditations for winning the lottery and you had somehow decided in your mind that that was actually a piece of the puzzle. In fact, it was an invented piece. You invented it and placed it into your picture. Now if I hadn't said anything, this piece would have become a piece of your reality. In other words, the picture you're painting will be different than the one I'm painting, even though we started off with exactly the same number and kinds of pieces. So the picture that you had painted with the pieces was real to you and it would have become the truth for you. But on the other hand the picture that I put together is true for me. In the same token it is the truth. So the real question remains: which is the truth and how does a person come as close as possible to the real truth?"

"I think I understand. What you're saying is still a little hazy in my mind though," he said.

"That's okay, just leave it that way. You actually want it on the hazy side. That way you're not creating another story out of a story."

"I've worked on this for many years. I was trying to understand the universe and how it works. But there was a basic problem that there are some things the mind is not able to deal with. For instance, trying to understand time or the concept of no time. They say that in fact everything happens simultaneously and that there is no such a thing as linear time. It's one thing to say that, but it's another thing to understand it. Very few people do understand it. It's like Einstein's theory of relativity. A lot of people have read some of it and don't really understand it, and there are people that have read it and think they understand it. But you can see by the research that they are doing that they have not understood what Einstein was trying to say. It's not a matter of brainpower, not at all. People have been taught that to understand complex things you have to be incredibly smart, but that's not true. Obviously I'm proof of that."

That got a chuckle out of Danny.

"So how is this going to help?" she asked.

"Give me a minute and I'll explain that. Sometimes it's hard for me to put things into words," I said, "Perhaps this will make sense to you. Years ago, I was trying to understand certain things and my brain was not able to deal with these theories, nor was I able to put them into a proper framework. About that time computers were just hitting the market and I found myself speaking to a salesperson who told me that the computer was not as important as the programs, because without the programs the computer is nothing more than a big paperweight. A light went on in my head. It's not that I'm too dumb, my brain is missing the program to understand certain things."

"So that's what this is, a program?" she asked.

"Yes."

"Sounds pretty simple for a program," Danny said.

"I agree, but brain programs are different than computer programs. The mind is a thousand times more complex than a computer and that allows the programs to be extremely simple. Things are kind of reversed but the idea behind it is the same.

"Okay, run it by me one more time."

"Take all the pieces of information you have and then separate them from each other. Break them into two or three pieces. The reason I say two or three pieces is that not all things consist solely of positive and negative. Some things and some pieces of knowledge also have a neutral aspect. Then put the pieces back together wherever they seem to fit the best but do not create or invent or guess at any other pieces. Most of all leave them slightly hazy. In other words, take certain pieces of information and don't completely accept them and don't completely reject them; just let them coast a bit. Sometimes pieces will be off to one side by themselves. If they do not fit, just leave them there. They will either be false information that you can discard, or later you will find a piece that will connect this piece to the rest. Let me give you an example of how to put the pieces together. We have future, angel, and winning. Two pieces fit together, and one piece stays off to one side. Of course, I'm talking about this story."

Danny thought for a moment. I looked towards Neena, but I already knew she had the answer.

"Okay," Danny said. "Future and angel fit, and winning belongs off to one side. I don't know why future and angel fit, but I know they do. I also have one other piece."

"What's that?"

"Something is not what it seems, and it belongs with future and angel. I'm missing the piece that ties them together, but I know they fit," he answered.

"You're right on the money. The program has to be used a bit before it really begins to kick in, but once it does, your mind will actually give you the pieces that you are missing. We know that everything is not as it appears so we leave future and angel as hazy, not totally accepting them as they appear and not totally rejecting them as they appear."

"Isn't that the same as guessing?" Danny asked.

"No, it's not, because when you're guessing you're using the same area of your mind that you would use if you were imagining things, but if you only look at the pieces that you have, your subconscious mind will begin to fill in the blank spaces. There's also a big difference between guessing or searching for more information."

"That's like saying that my mind already has the answers," Danny said.

"Exactly. Your mind does have the answer. The minute you ask a question, if the subconscious part of your mind does not already have that information it will immediately begin to find the information. And it can get those answers from various places from your soul or from your subconscious. There are various other places that the subconscious is connected to that can also give it information. The biggest problem is that subconscious cannot give the information to your conscious mind unless there is a program in place that can handle the information. The conscious mind and the subconscious mind do not communicate very well. Dreams are a good example and can be a real problem to decipher because the subconscious is trying to pass information to the conscious mind but the conscious mind is not able to deal with the information. So the subconscious uses symbols, which is a very primitive and crude method of communication."

Danny wiped his forehead. "That makes sense, but if I were to say there seems to be a barrier between the conscious mind and the subconscious mind, would I be correct?"

"Absolutely. That barrier needs to be there, but it doesn't need to be as thick as it is. The fact that the barrier is there allows the conscious mind to deal with just the moment and not all the other stuff that may be going on. Your subconscious mind, for example, hears everything, every single sound in the room, but consciously we only hear that which we focus on. The subconscious is like a filter that separates the things that perhaps are important to us from those things that are not. Besides, there is so much going on in the subconscious that when you get in there it's like sticking your head into a beehive."

I looked at them. "Mind you, I could be totally wrong. It wouldn't be the first time."

Defiant

By defiant
Defy that part of you
That says you can't
Defy it
And you will achieve it.

Chapter Fifteen

I realized that we were getting sidetracked again when Danny suggested we get back to the story.

"OK, so where did I leave off? Oh, yeah, I remember." I said. "I woke up the next morning in my usual wide awake death state. Actually I think it was more towards noon. My dog Rudy was sitting there staring at me. I was a little disappointed in him, because it seems every time the shit hits the fan he's nowhere to be found."

"Is he a male?" Neena smirked at me. I ignored her.

"I remember dragging myself out of bed and heading down the hallway. I took a peek in the living room. The coast was clear, so I headed for the shower. I was totally exhausted. I tried to go over some of the dreams I had but there were so many and all of them seemed to have this angel in them, at least the ones that I partially remembered. I felt like I had just relived ten years of childhood. In my dreams it appeared that this angel's name was Sneaky and according to the dreams, apparently we were friends. Normally I don't have a problem with dreams. I tend to just ignore them, but these were somehow mixing with my memories, at least the memories that I now seemed to have. I need to tell you, this was a very difficult period for me, and it's hard to remember every detail because it was very confusing."

"Anyway, after breakfast I decided to go to the store to pick up a few things. I took Rudy with me because he loves to ride in the car. On the way to the store there was this strange rhyme that kept replaying itself in my head like a musical tune…'Love is like the Book of Love.' I had no idea what that was supposed to mean or why it was there. I tried to ignore it and concentrate on separating my dreams from my memories. But by this time I was not even sure whether I had really seen an angel or perhaps just dreamed it. The thought that I might be losing my marbles had definitely occurred to me. I also thought that maybe something had gone wrong with my meditation, not that I have ever heard of anything going wrong before, but you never know."

"I found a parking spot very close to the door and told Rudy to stay in the car. The top was down on the convertible and it's not a lot of restraint for Rudy, especially if he spots a cat. I don't know, but there must be some kind of past life grudge between dogs and cats."

As I wandered around collecting some groceries I noticed that people were staring at me. As soon as I would look at them they would smile just like someone does when they know you. I looked at my pants, my shirt, and even looked at a reflection of myself in one of the glass doors, but I could see nothing out of place. If I stayed in one spot too long, people would start making conversation. People were also touching me, even if they weren't talking to me. They would pass by me and literally put their hand on my shoulder or arm. One woman was standing so close to me that anyone would have thought we were a couple, considering our bodies where most definitely touching. I tried to move over but that didn't seem to make any difference to her at all. She just simply moved her body along with mine. Normally you can go in there dragging a dead horse in and no one would notice. They would just keep their distance. This is one of those Mercedes Benz upper-class yuppie type grocery stores, and conversations are usually hidden behind sunglasses."

"This was too weird for me so I grabbed my basket and headed for the cashier, where things became even more bizarre. Even in the line at the cashier people were looking at me. If I looked back then they'd smile and sometimes move their lips as if to say hi, at which point I would immediately look away. As the line moved closer to the cashier the two women that I was standing in-between continued to move closer. You're not going to believe this, but the woman behind me was standing so close that I could feel her breath on my neck and we were making physical contact. The only time people stand this close is when they're in a serious relationship."

"Why didn't you just move forward?" Danny asked. Neena was laughing to herself.

"I tried, but the woman in front of me was actually backing up closer to me. I was also getting a little scared. Then the line moved forward, which meant she had to move, and at that point I put my basket between us. That solved part of the problem, at least until I had to put the basket down. By the time we reached the cashier we were so physically close that the cashier thought we were together."

"What would you have done if one of the ladies said yes when the cashier asked if you were all together?" Neena asked, obviously thoroughly enjoying this.

"Why didn't you talk to them? Chicken!" Danny said.

"Well, I can't really deny that. But I don't talk much even when I'm around people I know. It's not that I'm shy, just that people are not interested in what I spend my time thinking about. Besides I hate small talk. I consider it a waste of time even though sometimes it fascinates me to watch people who are masters at it. It's just a matter of perspective. Some people like myself want to take life apart and study it in order to figure out the universe. Others just want to live life, and many just want to survive it. Some people just do not want to discuss or think about whether plants have a consciousness and how it thinks. How about dolphins? Some people say that dolphins have a more sophisticated language then we have. Theoretically that would mean that they discuss things in a more minute detail, yet their life's seems simple compared to ours, which leads me to believe that there is more going on with them then we can see."

"I have an idea. How about getting back to the story?" Danny suggested.

"I guess so," I answered. "You know, to me telling this story is rather slightly boring. I have already lived it and went over it a thousand times in my mind. To me it's not that interesting anymore. Now, dolphins…there's an interesting conversation we could have."

"You never know," Neena said. "You might find something that you have missed."

"You might be right," I said. I thought about that for a minute. "Anyway, as I stepped out of the grocery store, I looked to see if Rudy was still in the car. He was, and so was that angel. From here on I'm just going to call him Sneaky because it will make it easier to tell the rest of the story, at least until the real truth comes out."

"Something deep inside of me turned. I didn't know whether to throw up again, or run, or maybe even just pretend this wasn't happening. Tears started to roll down my face. I really have no idea why. There was a woman approaching and she must have seen the tears on my face. She walked right up and tried to hug me, and I jumped back. She apologized and went into the store."

"Wow, so not only am I going to win lotteries, but I'll also turn into a chick magnet." Danny interrupted me with a smile that could have humbled a frog.

"Not quite," I said. "Now what did I tell you about jumping to conclusions?"

"So I won't be a chick magnet?" Danny gave me a disappointed look.

"You'll attract your share of ladies; not just women, but all people." I laughed. "This has nothing to do with the instructions I have given you. It has to do with Love. We'll get into that pretty soon. Anyway! Getting back to the story, Sneaky turned his head and looked right at me. He smiled and yelled, 'Do you want to drive or shall I drive?' I looked at Rudy and he seemed to be OK. His ears were up, which is usually a good sign. So I did the only thing I could do, given the options of either standing at the door crying or getting in the car."

"I'll try to replay the conversation we had on the way home." I said, grinning. "But before I forget, let me give you a little piece of advice you might want to hang onto for future reference."

"Never let an angel drive!"

They laughed. I took the opportunity to wet my palate with a little more scotch before continuing.

"Think about this for a minute." I put my glass on the bar. "What would you say to an angel sitting in your car? What would you do? Who would you tell? Who would believe you? Either my mind was in shock or it was overloaded because the only thing I could think of saying was, 'How many wishes do I get?'"

"Sneaky answered with something like, 'Boy, this is going to take longer than I anticipated. Do I look like I just slid out of an old jar? I'm an angel, not a genie. The reason I'm here is to help you put Love back into your life. To help you fulfill your dreams."

"Well, that's nice," I answered. "But I dream of money."

"You actually dream of having more Love, joy and freedom in your life. You just think that money will give this to you. And you're welcome."

"I don't remember saying thank you."

"You will."

"What does Love have to do with anything?" I asked.

"Everything!"

"Like?"

"Like no Love, no life. Love is the essence of life. Love is the essence of what you are. Love is the reason you are here. Love is everything. Love encompasses all there is and ever was and will be."

"I remember thinking to myself, 'I don't know why we're having this conversation. I'll just keep him talking until I figure a way out of this.'"

"You're nuts!" I told him. "You can't live without money, but you can live without Love."

"Is that so? Show me something that lives that has absolutely no Love. You can survive with very little Love, but you cannot live. There is a difference. A lack of Love does an enormous amount damage to a person and a person lacking in Love can and many times will do a lot of damage to others. People who start wars are a prime example. When you are filled with Love you do not send people to kill each other."

"I stopped at the red light and turned my head towards Sneaky. "What does this have to do with me?" At the same time I realized I was face to face with a police officer sitting in the car next to me. Something you do not want to do is to talk to an invisible angel while stopped at a red light next to a police car. Especially if you are driving in an open convertible."

"Did you get a little ride to the funny farm?" Danny laughed.

"No, I was lucky, but from the look on the police officer's face, it was a close one. I put my hand over my mouth and said, 'Wait until we get home.' I was thinking about what Sneaky said when it dawned on me that I had forgotten to pick up the information for the games playing today."

"Feeling lucky today, are you?" he asked.

"While maneuvering away from the police car, I asked him how he knew what I was thinking."

"Easy. I'm an angel. I know what you're thinking even before you do. It's part of the package."

"By the way, Danny, don't bother playing poker with angels. They cheat."

"I have a feeling that you might be right." Danny said.

"'OK, what am I thinking now?' I asked him."

"'You're hoping that I'll go to the casino with you.'"

"That's amazing." I turned into the driveway. Ideas were definitely rolling around in my head, like if you can't beat them, have them join you."

"'I don't suppose you know tomorrow's lottery numbers?' I asked. He didn't answer. I thought he must have a ticket or two stashed in those feathers somewhere, just waiting for a special occasion.

"'Every day is special.' he said."

"I turned to see if he had any pockets but he was gone."

Danny had a very puzzled look on his face.

"What's going on in that brain of yours, Danny?" Neena laughed.

"I'm trying to figure out what this angel was up to. I think another piece to the puzzle is Love. But he is definitely up to something." Danny said.

"Yup, he sure was."

Reading between the lines

Reading between the lines is something that I stumbled across many years ago. It's been extremely helpful. I'm going to make this short and sweet because sometimes simple is the best. The biggest problem with our language is that when we try to explain things like the universe, time, space, dimensions and consciousness, the words are just not there. But as life would have it, there always seems to be someone who finds a way around the limitations. The best way that I can explain it is that each word, written or spoken, seems to have a vibration and something else, which I can't explain because I don't really know what it is. Nevertheless, by putting certain words next to each other, they begin to vibrate differently Each word begins to vibrate to a different note, but also the two words together have a vibrating note also. But the most bizarre thing is, in any normal sentence with a certain amount of words in it, each word will vibrate and the sentence itself will also vibrate. Those notes do not change unless you change some of the words. There are sentences that are totally different, in which each word vibrates and the sentence vibrates, but not on a single note. It's almost like the sentence itself is singing a note that is telling a story beyond what is actually written.

I would Love nothing more than to explain to you how this works, but unfortunately I have no idea. However, I do know how to read between the lines, or to be more accurate, I know how to get my subconscious to give me the information.

Let me give you an example that you may have already experienced. Have you ever read something, a book or magazine, and after awhile suddenly you snapped out of the dream-like state and realized that even though you have read several pages, you have no idea what you have just read? It's like you were on automatic pilot. Part of you was reading and another part was daydreaming or at least something similar to that. While you were reading you came across one of these sentences and also at the same time you were probably in the correct mental state and your subconscious began trying to give you the information that the sentence is carrying. If your subconscious is giving you the information in symbols then the whole thing may appear almost like a dream and will have some parts of your reality mixed in which then you will need to separate.

Reading between the lines is one thing. To write between the lines is a totally different thing. I believe there are probably only a few people in the world that knows how to write this way. It would probably take a lifetime to learn. From the information that I have gathered, it appears that the highest concentration of people able to do this would come from Tibet. Language does not seem to matter. Even if you can't read the language you still can read between the lines. Actually the easiest way to learn it is to try to read a book in a different language. Of course it needs to be a book that was written in this form, any spiritual books or information written in Tibetan will work perfectly. This is how I learned it myself. I believe that the conscious mind becomes bored with trying to read something it can't, and at some point the subconscious takes over. You will most likely find that you will slip in and out of a dream state. Afterwards you need to look at your dream and even write it down so that you can analyze it afterwards. What you will find will knock your socks off. Another way that you can learn and practice this is to let yourself drift while reading. The best time to do this is usually the second time you read it. Of course, if you drift into your day-to-day concerns you will need to bring yourself back. My favorite way to do this is to pretend that a part of me is talking to me. I consider this part my subconscious. While I'm reading I drift back and forth. I read, then I listen, then I read and so on. Surprisingly enough, it's a lot easier than it sounds.

There are many books on the market that have information written between the lines. The interesting part is that even though people do not know how to write between the lines, it still seems to happen to writers who either channel or spend a lot of time meditating, especially if they meditate just before they start writing. Also I've noticed that in any books that have been translated from Tibetan to English by anyone who has mastered some degree of meditation, it appears that the information that is written in between the lines transfers itself over to the new language. I find this phenomenon mind-boggling. A perfect example is any book written by Alice A. Bailey. There is so much information between the lines that it could easily take four to five months just to get through one book. Other books you can take a look at are books by Seth, Sanaya Roman, Richard Bach, and many more. The amount of information written between the lines varies from book to book, although in the last few years it appears that it is happening more often.

The next time someone writes you a letter, you might want to try doing the same thing. Sometimes people write one thing and think another. For some reason what they were thinking shows up between the lines.

Now doesn't this sound like it could make some interesting reading?

There is a reason why I have given you this information at this particular point in the book. I could tell you, but that would take all the fun out of it.

Chapter Sixteen

"Let's get back to the story. Otherwise, this will take all night."

"I'm not sure how long it was exactly, but over the next few days I tried to sort out the memories of my childhood. I also tried to separate my dreams from my memories but there was no separating them. The whole thing was very confusing. I have a very good memory and I forget very little. It was hard for me to accept that I could forget several years of my life, especially the things that I now remembered. I remember having no friends and what seems like almost all my time was spent with this angel. I was not very well liked, actually more like despised. That's easy to understand when you're spending a lot of time talking to someone that no one else can see." I paused as I remembered how it had been.

"In one way I was hoping that I wouldn't see him again. Yet for the first time in a long time I felt lonely. I actually in some way wanted him to come back."

I took a drink from my glass. "You know, there's no way to explain what something like this does to you, especially if you can't even tell anybody about it. I guess it doesn't really mater now."

Neena reached over and rubbed my back. "You're not alone tonight."

"I guess..." I smiled.

"I'm pretty sure that it was Friday afternoon. I was sitting in my favorite chair by the window looking over the sports odds for the weekend. I wasn't sure whether I should try another meditation. After all, no one said that I shouldn't do this. But at the same time there was still a little concern in my mind whether I was really seeing an angel. If I'm seeing an angel who isn't really there, that could mean I've flipped out. If that were the case, I wouldn't be able to make a sane judgment whether this is real. About the same time I was thinking this, a flash of light caught my attention. I cautiously peeked out the window so I would not be spotted if it happened to be a reflection from a bill collector's car."

"'Didn't you already pay off all your bills with the money that you won?' Danny asked."

"Not even close. At that time in my life it would have taken a lot more money than I had won to financially balance everything out. I already would have increased the size of the bets but as you can see, things were getting a little hectic. Anyway, getting back to the story, as I peeked out the window I saw there were no cars or any sign of anyone. I turned back towards my tickets with a sigh of relief and almost jumped out of my chair. Sneaky was sitting on the sofa."

"'So I see you're working on your bets, peeking out the window, hiding from the bill collectors. Oh, what a tangled web we weave,' he said, using one of my favorite lines."

"I told him not to sneak up on me like that. As far as I'm concerned, even a hallucination should knock."

"'I tried to warn you, but you seemed too preoccupied with peeking,' he responded."

"Nobody's perfect."

"We both just sat there for a while in silence staring at each other. He must have known that I was trying to formulate my questions. I had a hundred of them yet I couldn't think of a single one. My mind was blank. Finally I managed to come up with something to ask."

"How do I know you're real?"

"'Trust!'"

"'What if I'm hallucinating?' I didn't realize just how stupid that question was. There's one sure way to know whether you've totally flipped out, and that's to ask a hallucination if you are hallucinating."

They both laughed, suggesting that I might be right.

"'Obviously you're not in shock now, so ask yourself this: what comes after shock?' Sneaky asked."

"I thought for a moment. 'After shock comes denial, or disbelief.' Right about then Rudy walked into the living room, looked over at Sneaky, then walked over to where I was sitting and laid down staring at the angel."

"'OK, if you're real, why didn't I remember you before the other day?' I asked."

"'But you did remember,' he said. 'You just assumed that you made it all up because it was hard for you to believe in something that did not fit into the world that you made for yourself.'"

"I didn't say anything, but I must have had a puzzled look on my face because somehow even though what he said could have been correct. I just didn't feel that it fit with me one hundred percent."

"You were also very young and a lot of very unpleasant things happened to you. When children go through difficult times, they tend to suppress some of their memories in order to continue to function. This is simply self-preservation."

"I knew he was right, but I still wasn't convinced."

Sneaky continued to try to convince me.

"'Unfortunately, memories tend to go in packages.' he said. 'As one memory is suppressed, others that can trigger this memory will also be suppressed. I became the trigger mechanism and as soon as you saw me you were faced with the reality that I must exist. It's your mind's job to make sense of what you see and in order for it to do this it looks for memories. One triggers the next in a domino effect."

"'Let me interrupt you for a moment,' Danny said. 'Did you have an angel for a friend when you were a kid or didn't you?'"

"That's the million dollar question, isn't it? I have my theories, but let's wait and see if you two come up with the same answers," I said.

"Something doesn't quite jive, but I can't put my finger on it yet." Neena observed. Danny nodded in agreement.

I took another sip from my Scotch. "I was sitting there and still couldn't think of any questions to ask. Thinking about it now, I find that rather strange. Then something came to my mind. 'Come to think of it, where the hell were you when the shit hit the fan? I could have used some help, not to mention a little company. Do you have any idea how much time and effort went into trying to get over all that?' At that moment I felt a lot of anger surging up. Rudy decided to go lie in a more serene area."

"'The way I remember it, you were quite adamant that I leave. Let me rekindle your memory. I think you said, and please correct me if I'm wrong...' he answered."

"'Never mind, I remember,' I interrupted him. 'I told you to go because I didn't want to have anything to do with Love anymore. I said people are cruel and everyone thinks I'm crazy and I blamed you for not having any friends. I said people don't care and because of you they're sending me away. I said you were wasting my time telling me things that no one cares about.'"

"After I said that to him. I remember falling into silence at the feelings that were coming up. When I was a kid I had started hating this world and the people in it. Survival! Survival was everything, more important than Love, more important than fun. Survival is all there is, I told myself. Survive until I'm bigger and stronger and then I'll fight back. Those are the thoughts I had when I was about eight years old."

"'Then you should have helped,' I said, 'instead of showing up now just when things are going good.'"

"'You were never alone,' he answered. 'No one is, even if they think they are. Ask yourself how many unexplainable things happened to you just when you needed it most?"

"Looking up towards the ceiling, I wondered how so many things can go wrong in one lifetime."

"He disappeared right after I looked away, which was just as well. I needed time to figure everything out."

I reached for my cigarettes and asked Danny if I could have some more orange juice.

"It's strange," I looked at Neena. "Even now that I'm telling you this, all the feelings are coming back as if it was yesterday. Don't you think that's strange?"

Neena shook her head. "No."

There were several long moments of silence before I continued with the story.

Hugs

Trees are the only ones I know
That like those Hugs.
You know,
The kind where you squeeze,
But a big squeeze.
I mean a really really big squeeze.
No not just big but really really really really big
The kind that makes your ears turn red
Now that's a Hug
Only trees like it that way, and me.

Chapter Seventeen

Danny jumped off his stool and poured me another glass of orange juice with a little bit of crushed ice.

"So you don't think there's anything wrong with using your method to win the lottery?" Neena asked.

Danny shook his head. "I don't see anything wrong with it."

"Isn't it like trying to get something for nothing?"

"I guess in some ways it is. But in other ways, you'd be putting a real effort into it, not just throwing your money into the wind hoping that luck takes over. You're using your mind and all the abilities that you have. You're also not taking anything from anybody else because if someone else has the right answers they'll win too.

"That's a good point," Danny said, "but what if you decide to write about this and too many people decide to do this? Pretty soon there won't be any lottery."

"I know what you mean. The bottom line is that it's already happening."

"What do you mean?" Neena asked. "What did you do?"

Danny's eyes were as big as watermelons again.

"Well, about six months ago I wanted to write a book telling the story of what happened. I didn't know how to write it so I took a tape recorder and just told the story, the same as I am telling you it now. It took about four tapes…almost six hours, and then I made copies and sold a bunch of them just to see if anyone was interested. Apparently a few people out there have taken it to the maximum because I heard that the Sports Lottery Commission is having a real problem balancing their books because suddenly there seems to be a group of people who are constantly winning. First they tried to lower the odds, hoping that this would break whatever system people were using, but it didn't. Now they have limited the amount of money that you can bet. I heard throughout the grapevine that the Lottery Commission is frantically trying to figure out what system these people are using. But the bottom line is, there is no system."

"How many tapes did you sell?" Neena asked.

"About a dozen."

"If you only sold one dozen, what will happen if you write a book and thousands of people read it?"

"It's hard to say. Maybe the Lottery Commission will have to shut down or find a way to make the game more challenging. It's a lot like playing chess. If you're not going to use your mind, there's no point in playing. The government has decided to make gambling legal for its own purposes, and if they're not willing to take the heat that comes with that kind of decision, then it's best for them to stay out of it. They seem to have no problem at all raking in millions of dollars from hard working individuals. Whether they're willing to give it back is not my concern. The world isn't going to end just because the lotteries are shut down. Besides, this story is not about money or the lottery. It's about Love and what you can do with Love and your mind."

"But if the lottery is shut down, learning this will be useless." Danny said.

"Not at all! There are an incredible amount of things that you can do with this talent. To think that you can only use it for winning the lottery is silly and narrow minded. There are many incredible and wonderful things that this method can be used for. You can use it to make a real difference in this world and to help a lot of people. You can use it at your job or in your business. It's endless! Just because the lottery may not be around, at least in the way it is right now, is no reason to hold this information back. The only reason I'm telling you about the lottery first is because that is how I started, then I slowly learned the rest, which you will find out about as soon as you let me get back to the story."

"Do that!" Danny said eagerly.

Neena leaned towards me. "Are you still playing the lottery?"

"No. Well maybe I shouldn't say no. I still play every now and then, mostly for fun. I throw in two dollars. It's very seldom when I don't win but as far as trying to make money with it, I stopped that a long time ago. Money was never really what I was after. I admit I got sidetracked for a while. What I was after was to be happy, and being happy in a way that doesn't depend on money or things or relationships or anything external. I'm happy to say that after 41 years I finally have achieved my goal. There is nothing that can compare with that. I am working on another project though, and I use the lottery to measure how well it's working. But that's another story."

"How did you achieve your happiness?" Neena asked.

"The rest of the story will explain that."

The Secret

Yesterday I asked my dog
What is your secret to life?
He answered
If it runs, chase it
I asked,
What if it doesn't run?
He answered
Just wait....

Chapter Eighteen

"Sunday is my favorite day," I said. "The streets are quiet and there are no bill collectors lurking around the corner. A good time to go for groceries. Rudy and I decided to brave it out and give that grocery store one more try. I told Rudy to stay in the car and as I walked in I thought the first sign of trouble, I'm out of there. I slowly worked my way around the store, unnoticed. Everything was back to normal. Boy, was that a relief! Walking around picking up a few more things I passed the stationery shelf, and a notebook fell off the shelf and right into my little red basket. You've got to admit the odds of having something like that happening are pretty low. Nevertheless, I picked up the book and flipped through the pages. A thought occurred to me: what if Sneaky doesn't show up for a while? I could end up forgetting everything. The first day was already fading; it seemed more like a dream. I put the notebook back on the shelf. But as soon as I got home I started making some notes."

"I was sitting in the living room on my favorite chair by the window writing when I heard a voice say, 'I'm glad to see that you've adjusted.'"

"I didn't need to look to know who it was. I said 'Gee, I wish you wouldn't sneak up on me like that! Why don't you knock on the front door?'"

"'You never answer the front door.'"

"'Okay, knock on the back door.'"

"'You don't answer that door either.'"

"'I guess you have a point. How about a flash of light just before?'"

"'That can be arranged.'"

"This time I was prepared. I already had written down some questions that I wanted to ask. I flipped the pages in my notebook.

"'Here's a question for you,' I said. 'What happened at the store the other day? People were acting very weird.'"

"'To put it mildly, you were glowing,' he smiled.

"What?"

"'Let me ask you this: what happens when people fall in Love?'"

"They glow."

"And?"

"'Give me a minute.' I was sure I had the answer. After all, I've seen it many times."

"'First they get this glow about them,' I said. 'Then they seem to become more attractive, especially to the opposite sex. They just seem to attract people.'"

"'Exactly. Try to look at it this way. When a person falls in Love their hearts start to open and they literally begin to radiate Love. This is what gives them that glow. And in your case the same thing happened. Your heart opened temporarily and you were radiating Love, only in much larger amounts than you are use to seeing.'"

"'Pretty dangerous stuff. Let's hope it doesn't happen again.' I shook my head.

"Sneaky was shaking his head too. 'Just imagine what you could do if you learned to open your heart, Klaus.'"

"'Yeah, just imagine what I could do with a million dollars, Sneaky.'"

"'Do you remember when you were six?' he asked. I shrugged my shoulders."

"'You wanted to know everything about Love. You wanted everyone to be happy. You wanted to change the world to make a difference. You would stand in the middle of a field pretending to send Love to all the flowers and butterflies like a little sun radiating with Love. Remember that?'"

"'Not really. After all, I was only six and obviously didn't realize what planet I was on. I'm getting a very strange feeling, like you're trying to trick me into doing something I don't want to do.'"

"'What is it that you don't want to do?'"

"I thought for a moment. 'You've got me there. I don't have a clue.'"

"'OK, what is it that you want to do?'"

"This was starting to give me a headache. I've been through this a thousand times in my mind and every time I find something that I think I would enjoy, doing it seems to fizzle out. I could sense that Sneaky heard my thoughts."

"'I just don't know,' I responded. 'It's like something is missing and I just can't seem to put my finger on it. Sometimes I think it's boredom, but that's not it. It's like...my life is like paint with no color in it.'"

"'Let's go back to when you were six or seven. Think about it. Did the things you did then seem to be colorless?'"

"I was trying to think. I grabbed a cigarette and while I was lighting it, I noticed out of the corner of my eye that Sneaky was gone."

I stopped a moment to take a drink of my orange juice.

"'So what did you do when you were younger? It sounds like you were happy then,' Neena said."

'Well...things were not the greatest. Actually most of the time it was barely bearable. But I had things I Love to do, stuff...you know, stuff you just can't get enough of. Every day I was raring to go. I couldn't wait to get out of the door. Sleep was something I did when I just couldn't keep my eyes open for even one more minute. After Sneaky left I thought about all of this. When I was younger, something was different inside me. When I was little, sleep was a nuisance, but later in my life sleep became an escape and there were many things on my list of stuff that just needed to go. But that still didn't bring me any closer to understanding what it was that made the difference. Whatever it was definitely seemed to be missing later on in my life."

"'So you still don't know what's missing?' Neena asked.

"'I do now, but at that time, when Sneaky first came around, I had no clue at all. Actually I had thought that the reason Sneaky was there had something to do with winning the lottery. But I was starting to realize that he hadn't come because of the lottery but for some other reason. That realization made me a lot more comfortable around him. I was a little less defensive after that. As far as what was missing in my life or in me, just hang in there, it's all in the story."

Danny breathed a sigh of relief. "So the reason he was there had nothing to do with the lottery, right?"

"That's right." I answered "But it does have something to do with the method."

I smiled as Danny's shoulders drooped. Neena seemed to think it was quite funny also.

I Am a Dog and This is My Life

I sleep
I dream
I make a cat or two run
For their lives
And the day is done.
What a glorious life
Perhaps tomorrow there will be a squirrel
Oh, yes, tomorrow…
A big fat slow-running squirrel.

Chapter Nineteen

I looked at Neena and Danny and asked, "Have you ever thought about how much effort and time goes into operating a physical body?" Both of them just gave me puzzled looks.

I shook my head. "It's like this. A few days after the last visit, I still hadn't made any bets, mostly because I was unsure of things. In some ways the possibility that I could have flipped out was still in my mind. I felt that the fact that I was still questioning myself gave me an indication that I was still all right."

"I was taking a bath, listening to ZZ Top with my headphones and contemplating the complexity of having a physical body and the complexity of life. Think about how much it takes to run a physical body from one day to the next. It's enormous! We get up in the morning, and the first thing we need to do is drain off excess fluid. Then we wash, scrub and comb our body. Then we spray, rub and squeeze some more stuff on it. But that's not all. Then we put on clothes that we had to wash, dry, press, and fold. Now at this point you'd think you're done, right? No, this is just the tip of the iceberg. So now it needs refueling, but nothing as simple as a bale of hay. We need to stir, percolate, mix, grill, and finally shove the whole thing into a hole in our heads, and don't forget to chew. Boy I Love efficiency. We need a place to store this body, especially at night so nothing will eat it while we're sleeping, and to keep it dry if it happens to rain.

So we rent, buy, or build a shelter. But in order to do this you take your body someplace and make it do things, and then someone gives you paper, which you give to somebody else. Now to go to this place where they give you paper when you make your body do things it does not want to do, you need body transportation devices which is like a body shell that you need to feed with a hose, and wash, wax, repair, and shelter. That makes sense, doesn't it? So now you need to do more building and paper trading. And to make matters even more bizarre, have you ever noticed that there is always something either trying to eat or mate with your body? Just take your body to the park and watch what happens. Bugs try to suck your blood; dogs try to lick your face off, and the next thing you know some other body tries to rub itself against yours. Go figure."

Danny and Neena were laughing quite hard by this time. Apparently they thought it was quite funny. Unfortunately back in those days I saw it as the truth and took it a lot more seriously. I lit another cigarette and waited patiently for Danny and Neena to settle down so I could continue.

"I was still in the tub. My eyes were closed, but I thought I saw a flash of light through my eyelids. Opening my eyes, I saw Sneaky sitting on the toilet holding a paper sailboat and a razor. My heart speeded up while I looked at the razor. It was an old one, the kind that opened at the top like the bomb doors on a B52 bomber. There was something familiar about those two things. I was just waiting for my memory to catch up."

"'I can see why you've lost some of your sense of humor, looking at life that way.' Sneaky said.

"'What?' I kept one eye on the razor and the other on the door."

"'What you where just thinking about.'"

"'Oh, just a thought, that's all.' I said."

"'No, I think it's more than that.' he said, giving me a concerned look. 'You see if you take Love out of life, everything becomes mechanical, cold and Loveless. It's true that a lot of the things you need to do are the same every day, but if there is Love in your actions, things have a certain romance to them. Take your bath, for instance. Basically it has one main function, but add a few bubbles, some toys…which I see you have, perhaps a candle and some pleasant conversation or even some music, and you have a totally new experience.'"

"'What's with the boat and razor?'"

"'You remember! Someone made you a paper boat just like this one because you didn't want to take a bath. My, how things change. I see you have plastic ones now. But as soon as you saw the paper boat, you rushed upstairs into the tub."

"'Yes, I remember.'"

"'Do you remember the razor?' Sneaky grinned as he pointed the razor at me.

"'Yes.' I answered. The memory had already clicked in my mind. 'It's hard to forget, considering I'm still sitting on the scar.'"

"'Do you remember me telling you not to play with this razor?'"

"'You were always telling me not to do this or that.' I said. 'So what's your point?'"

"'There is no way to prove to you that I am real and that you are not crazy. Everything can be considered a fragment of your imagination; it's not for me to do it for you, but for you to trust yourself for in that lies a great achievement. So think about what has been missing in your life all these years.'"

"I looked up. 'Why don't you just tell me?'"

"But he was already gone. He did leave the paper sailboat. As I grabbed it I noticed there was some writing on its side: Several years ago you imagined doing something. Remember, for your thoughts create reality. Proof is the burden of the disbeliever.'"

I plunked the sailboat into the water, put my headphones on, and played with it, at least until it sank. It brought back a lot of memories. But I couldn't figure out what I had imagined two years ago that is now supposedly reality."

I knew what Neena wanted to ask.

Here's a riddle

Are you ready?
Okay then!
Conscious creation.
Is a Conscious Creation?
(I never said that it was going to be an easy one.)

Chapter Twenty

Danny looked at his notebook and rubbed his forehead. Neena noticed Danny's expression also, and asked him what was wrong. He just mumbled something, but didn't really answer. I was pretty sure I knew what was going on in his head.

"What's the matter, Danny?" I asked. "Having conflicting beliefs?"

Danny looked up at me. "What do you mean?"

"Come on. It's written all over your face. You're not sure what to believe anymore and whether this lottery thing will work. Right?"

"I guess so," he answered. "I'm not saying that you're not telling the truth. It's just that maybe it works for you, but that doesn't mean it will work for me."

"If ten angels came here right now directly from God and told you it will work for you, would you believe it then?"

"Most definitely." Danny's eyes gleamed.

"How about if it was just one big fat beer-burping angel? Would it work for you then?"

Neena chuckled.

"Possibly."

"Why would it make a difference to you how many angels there are?"

"I don't know. I guess it just makes it more believable." Danny shook his head. "I don't get what you're trying to tell me."

"The bottom line is that you're right, it won't work for you."

Danny had a shocked look on his face, and so did Neena. For a second I thought Danny was going to lose it.

"The reason it won't work for you is because you don't believe it, so tell me why you believe that it will not work for you."

Danny thought for a moment. "I guess it seems too simple. You'd think that with all the millions of people on this planet, somebody would have figured it out before."

"Logically that makes perfect sense, and at one time I too actually believed that. Later I realized that it was just my limiting belief trying to justify itself. I'm not the only one that has done this. It's just that everyone else who has also achieved this is being very quiet about it. It's very strange but as soon as you discover something it seems that other people who have also discovered it seemed to come out of the woodwork."

"Beliefs are locked doors, or keys that open any door," Neena observed.

"That's true," I said. "Right now your beliefs are locked doors. If we convinced you that you could not learn to ski and you believed it, then you would not learn to ski. That's just the way it is, even if all the evidence proves the opposite."

"But if something is proven, then it's real and we should believe it."

"No!" I shook my head.

Danny grabbed his empty glass and slammed it on the bar in front of me. "This glass is round. I believe it."

I grabbed the glass and threw it on the floor behind the bar. It smashed into a thousand pieces.

"No, the glass was round on the sides, but flat on the bottom and hollow in the top. Now it's none of those things." I realized it was a lousy example.

"I can't prove to you how your beliefs affect everything that you can or can't do. Years ago I took some courses. One was a meditation course, another was a mind power course, and a third had to do with utilizing the power of the subconscious. At some point in all three courses one person asked this question: can I use this to win the lottery or in the stock market? Each time they were told 'no' in a few different ways. And to be honest, for awhile I even believed that myself. But then I got suspicious because they tell you that you can do all kinds of incredible things, but not that one. Everybody seems to steer you away from it. It becomes especially interesting when you see that very same person buying a lottery ticket. What they're telling you is that you are allowed to buy a lottery ticket but not allowed to use all the resources that you have available to you to make that piece of paper worth anything. Winning the lottery has turned out to be my smallest achievement but my biggest step because I finally got it through my thick skull that I am not a helpless little thing that God has forgotten about. I can do anything that I believe I can. I'm going to show you something tonight that will do far more for you than the lottery ever will, and if you use it you won't need the lottery."

I helped him clean up the broken glass and then continued with the story.

"I had just gone to bed and closed my eyes when I noticed a flash of light. I knew who it was. Slightly turning my head and opening one eye, I could see Sneaky sitting on the edge of my bed."

"'Why didn't you come before I went to bed?' I asked him."

"'I thought you might like a bedtime story, like when you were little.'"

"'I remember your bedtime stories and the way I remember them, they were more like lectures.'"

"I knew he was up to something; I could feel it."

"'They always made you fall asleep and have good dreams, didn't they?'"

I looked at Neena and then at Danny. "By the way, have you noticed something strange about the way Sneaky talks?" They shook their heads.

"Come on now, he talks exactly the way I do. He uses the same words and has the same speech patterns. Don't you find that strange?"

"'I thought that it was just the way you were telling the story.' Neena said."

"'Not at all. You might want to keep that in mind. Anyway let's get back to where I left off.'"

"I agreed to listen to Sneaky's bedtime story, laid back, and closed my eyes."

"'Once upon a time there was a little boy whose only friend was an angel. All their time was spent together playing, laughing, sword fighting, climbing trees, and talking about making the world a better place, full of Love and fun. Many of their days were spent searching for treasure at the garbage dump. Of course the angel always found the best treasure.'"

"'Many of their days were spent on the lake in a small rowboat, where they could talk for hours without anyone hearing them. They would ride the big waves that the larger boats made and laugh. The boy was happy there. One day the little boy told his angel friend to leave and never come back. The boy said 'Because of you, everyone hates me and they think I'm stupid and crazy.' This was a sad day for both of them. But what the boy did not know was that when he angrily sent the angel away he also turned his back on Love. Not allowing any Love into his physical being nor believing in Love created more and more pain. This pain grew as he got older. The boy, now a man, tried many things to fix what was wrong but he did not know he was starving from a lack of Love. And no matter how much Love the angel sent, the Love would not go in, for his heart was closed.'"

"Sneaky paused for a moment."

"'Now the angel never actually left the boy's side but just made himself invisible, because the angel knew that someday the boy would change his mind. Sure enough, years later he did. And together again, they decided to write a book about Living on Love.'"

"'You're dreaming, buddy. I'm not telling anybody anything.' I tried to ignore him and let myself drift into sleep. I only remember what I faintly heard."

"'One day the boy, now a man, won the lottery and with that money he purchased a nice cabin in the woods where he spent much of his time writing about Love and the reality of life. One day as the man was walking in the woods he saw a girl talking to the trees.'"

"'They say the boy who talks to angels and the girl who talks to the trees lived happily ever after.'"

"'Forget that. How much did I win?' I asked, not sure whether it was out loud or just in my head."

"He must have moved closer. I was just at the point of dozing off when I heard him loud and clear."

"'Dreams create believers and believers create. You may want to watch for the tent, and the spots on her back. She obviously knows you very well, otherwise she would not need to make it that obvious.'"

Neena almost busted her gut laughing. Danny followed with his own tears of laughter. I had to laugh a little myself even though I didn't think it was that funny. I wasn't even sure exactly what Neena thought was so funny. I thought, 'she knows something I don't.' She managed to get herself under control for a few seconds and then she would break out in laughter again. This went on for quite a while. I couldn't help laughing myself just watching her laugh.

"You men are all the same." Neena wiped the tears from her eyes. I was holding my stomach because it was hurting from laughing so hard.

"You couldn't see a stick in the mud if you tripped over it," she said in a condescending tone. "Just imagine at some time before you were born you both decided to meet up sometime during your lifetime. Just to make sure that you would be able to get it through your thick skull, she felt she needed to put a sign on her back so that there was no chance of you missing it."

She still had a big grin on her face. I was trying to find a way to fire back. I looked at Danny.

Danny looked at her. "Why should it be up to him? Maybe if she got her act together she'd be able to find him." I thought it was a good response and nodded my head.

"You men are so blind that you couldn't see her even if you tripped over her." She broke out in laughter again. There was no sign at all that she was trying to hold it back, so Danny and I decided to have our own conversation.

"You haven't by chance found her?" Danny tried to say it loud enough so I could hear him over Neena's laughter, which made her laugh ever harder.

"I think I have. There are still some questions that I haven't totally worked out yet."

"So you've seen her, but haven't actually met her?" he asked.

"Something like that. It's been over two years since Sneaky told me that bedtime story. At that time I wasn't interested, but later on I started wondering about the implications of what he had told me."

Danny had a puzzled look on his face. Neena had settled down but was still grinning from ear to ear.

"So now we come to the chicken parts." She was obviously enjoying this to the utmost.

"It's not that. I don't know exactly how to explain it, but our future, our present, and our past are never complete. They can be changed at any time. I know this sounds strange and in some ways impossible but towards the end of the story there is a really good example. Now just for a minute accept the possibility that as we live our lives we have the ability to change our life experience. A lot of it has to do with what we fully believe. For instance, take Danny winning the sports lottery. It may or may not be in his life experience as it is set in place right now but if he believes that it is possible, he switches into a new probability and is able to play the sports lottery the way I showed him, and win."

"What does that have to do with this woman?"

"When Sneaky first said this to me, I ignored it. Later I started thinking about it and in a sense also began believing it for various reasons, perhaps because I wanted to. I started searching around in different probabilities and I found her. Then I found her here in the physical probability, or the physical experience that I am in now. Actually she's a lot closer than I expected. But there are still of unanswered questions. To find her in the first place, instead of traveling into the future, I traveled in the present and probable present realities, which I will explain later. I went back several times. Sometimes she seemed to be there and other times not. Was she actually there or did she get placed there in this probability after Sneaky made the suggestion and I accepted the belief? This is exactly what causes the physical experiences that we experience. Beliefs are directly linked to our physical experience."

Neena was shaking her head as Danny said, "That's confusing as hell but I still don't see why that has anything to do with whether you actually go and talk to her."

"It's complicated." I shook my head. "When Sneaky made that suggestion it doesn't mean that it was the reality at the time. He may have just flung that reality at me. Just because it has become a part of my physical reality or experience doesn't mean it is part of hers."

Neena touched her cheek. "You might be right! Two stubborn thick-sculled people in the same room at the same time could cause some complications. Especially if she is as big a chicken as you are."

"So how did you manage to find her in real life?" Danny asked.

"Actually I've known her for over twenty years. The problem is that I have conflicting information. This could be just be his twisted way of getting me to spend more time studying time and probable events."

"Just thinking about this is giving me a headache. Can I have another scotch?" I asked.

"Sure, no problem." Danny chuckled to himself.

One Battle Too Many

I have been a warrior
For as long as I can remember.
I have stood my ground,
I have fought the universe, God and country
And the dragons inside.
I am so good
At times I have even cut myself
Ouch
And as the last warrior in me
With a tear in his eye
Lays down his sword
I ask, now what?

Chapter Twenty-One

"The next morning I woke up in a good mood. Dreaming about winning has a tendency to put me in a more receptive mood in the mornings.

Still lying in bed, I was thinking about what to do today when I noticed a soft glow coming from the hallway. I was hoping it was the sun coming up but I could see from my window that it was cloudy. Sometimes you know it's going to be a long day just by how it starts."

"I slid out of bed and staggered down the hallway. Sneaky was waiting for me in the kitchen."

"'Have a good sleep?' he asked."

"'I guess so, I think I did.' I rubbed my eyes."

"'You might want to tell that to your face, it doesn't seem to be aware of that.'"

"'Very funny.' I opened the fridge to see if there were any eggs left."

"'So, where do you want to start today?' he asked."

"'I want to start with breakfast that's where, so back off. I need time to ease myself back into the world.'"

"'Boy, talking to you in the morning is like grabbing a bear by the lips!'"

"I didn't respond. About that same time Rudy came in through his doggy door and the two of them sat in the kitchen and minded their own business while I finished making breakfast. I put my toast on my plate and set the plate on the table, and gave Rudy his usual half slice of toast. Not that he ever eats it; he just licks the butter off. Rudy took his toast and went outside while I sat down to eat my breakfast. Sneaky just sat there staring. Finally I gave in."

"'OK, I'd rather listen to you talk then sit there burning holes in my eggs with your staring.' I said."

"'I was just wondering if you were going to put some Love in your food?' He asked with a smirk on his face."

"I put my fork down and rolled my eyes. 'What's the point of that? I'm just going to eat them anyway and so it will come right back. Besides I have no idea what the hell you're talking about.'"

"'When you send Love into your food when you're preparing it or just before eating it, it's absorbed by the food and in many ways changes it, increasing the life energy and even improving the taste. The cells in your body are able to absorb this Love, and food filled with Love has a lot of healing properties. You'll find it easier to digest, it will give you more energy, and you'll find it more calming, but most of all you'll be adding Love directly to your physical body.'"

"A thought occurred to me about the same time that he said this. What if he had something to do with the fact that I was having trouble getting the correct game results and therefore not doing very well with my sports lottery wins? Perhaps I should play along just in case."

"'I have no idea how to do this,' I answered. 'I've never read anything about this or heard anyone mention sending Love into your food."

"'That's because people are not yet aware of the power of Love or how it can be used. Love is one of the most powerful things in the universe. Would you agree with this?'"

"I nodded and said, 'I guess so, but that doesn't help anything because whoever or whatever controls and directs Love doesn't seem to be around.'"

"'But you are around; actually several billion of you. People have the ability to send Love, massive amounts of Love, to anything and anywhere. Think of the possibilities! Let's start with your eggs.'"

"'Look! I just want to eat my breakfast, so whatever it is you want me to do, just tell me and let's get on with it.' I started to get a little irritated."

"Now we're getting to the interesting stuff." Neena said.

"I agree, this is what the whole story is about, but it gets better."

"Can you use Love for the lottery?" Danny grinned from ear to ear.

"Probably, but I'm not really sure. I know you can use it for money, but I'll explain that later."

"So what happened next?" Neena asked.

"'Just close your eyes and use your imagination to follow my directions.' Sneaky said. 'It's not important that you have your eyes closed. It will just be easier for you until you get the feel of it.'"

"I closed my eyes, relaxed, and followed his instructions."

"'Just imagine that there is a light in your upper chest near your heart and imagine it growing brighter and brighter, radiating with Love. Breathe slowly and deeply, filling your lungs with air. Breathing is important. Now let the light have a nice steady glow, like the glow you see from a candle, only much larger. Let it become more radiant and begin to surround your whole body. That's it, the sensation you're getting in your chest is all right, that is your heart opening. Now imagine sending a beam of Love from this glowing area to the food on your plate. Good. When you sense it is enough, then just let go and open your eyes, bringing yourself back into the present moment. There you go.'"

"I opened my eyes and said, 'That was easy. Are you sure this makes a difference?'"

"'More than you can imagine, my friend. One day there will be restaurants and coffee shops specializing in food that are filled with Love. Food that is filled with Love will do more for you than any food you now might consider health food.'"

"I had started eating again while Sneaky was babbling away."

"'Hey, this seems to taste better. It's almost like it has more flavor! Are you sure this isn't my imagination?"

"'Absolutely! When scientists discover that Love has a physical form and that it actually has a particle that exists everywhere at the same time. It won't take long for them to figure out that the amount of Love in the food is directly linked to its life energy and its healing and life sustaining qualities. And that's only the tip of the iceberg.'"

"'Interesting.' I said."

"'If you do the same thing to your food before putting it away, you will find that it also keeps much longer.'"

"When I looked up from my plate he was gone. I washed my dishes and sat down in my favorite chair in the living room."

"I'm going to have to try this out," Neena looked at Danny. "Would you please get me a small glass of orange juice?"

"Good idea." Danny poured her orange juice.

"Okay, let me see." Neena sipped her orange juice and closed her eyes. Danny and I watched in anticipation. I smoked my cigarette while Neena sent Love into her glass.

She opened her eyes and took a sip of her orange juice, and then another before she put the glass down.

"You know what? I think it works! It seems to taste more orange, more like it was freshly squeezed."

"It definitely does make a difference," I said, "I've played with this over the last two years and had some really interesting results. I'll give you some examples. The day after Sneaky told me about this; I was going to a farewell party for a friend. Each of us had to bring some kind of food to the party and I decided to try a little experiment. The next morning, I went to the bakery and bought some cookies. I put them on two identical plates, then I marked the bottom of one plate with a felt marker, and spent about 15 to 20 minutes sending Love to the cookies on that one plate. I figured if a little bit is good then a whole lot more will be better, which is not always correct when it comes to Love. I took both plates to the party and set them both side by side on the table. When people started eating the cookies they reached for the ones that I had sent Love to first! Two people reached over the other plate to get to the plate of cookies that I had sent Love to. All the cookies were eaten because they were very good cookies, but the ones that I had sent Love to were gone long before anyone started on the ones on the other plate."

"That's really interesting. Did you try anything else?" Neena asked.

"Over the years I've done a lot of experiments like this at different parties. The results are always the same. Even if I didn't bring the food I noticed that the minute I take something and send Love to it people seem to immediately go for it without ever knowing what's going on. Sometimes when I go to a restaurant I don't wait for the food to get to my table before I send Love. I do it as soon as I order it. I also send Love to the waitress and to the cook. This really makes a big difference. Many times I get a huge plate of food…even though someone else orders the same thing, they just get a small amount on their plate while mine is literally heaping over. Many times I get my food faster and sometimes before others who ordered before me. All kinds of interesting things happen every single time. If I don't send Love, then everything basically stays normal and many times is less than satisfactory, even though I'm not very fussy. Once you start to see these little miracles and get used to them, you seem to miss them when they're not there. When I don't send Love, it feels and tastes like something is missing. You'll just have to try it for yourself. It really doesn't take much effort."

"What if I were to send Love to the food before I serve it to someone?" Danny asked.

"That's a good question. The thing about Love is that it's unpredictable. You'll never know exactly what the results will be. So you'll just have to try it and see for yourself. But I can tell you that you will be pleasantly surprised and you will also probably have a return customer."

"Can I do this with drinks?" Danny asked.

"Of course, and you should. From here on I rather expect it."

Love

Ever so slightly she said, I could easily fall in Love with you
I said thank you but will you Love all parts of me?
What do you mean? She asked
If you open your heart to all there is, all life
All experiences, all people, and to yourself
Then you will actually be in Love.
And no matter what I have done or not done
Will do or not do, will be or not be
Your heart will always be open
And perhaps in time my heart will learn to do the same.
At this she turned away, swearing never to return
But I know differently.
For Love has a soul mate named Trust
And at times they seem to be apart
But this is only an illusion
For they are inseparable.

Chapter Twenty-Two

"Sneaky didn't show up for at least four or five days, which gave me the opportunity to go back to my betting and daily routine. After a few days I was getting pretty frustrated. It was taking an enormous amount of time and effort and I wasn't getting the results that I wanted or what I had before. Even though I know now what the problem was, at that time I had no clue. Problems aren't hard to solve if you know what is causing them, but if you can't see it even though it's right in front of you, you're sort of like a pickle in a jar."

"I forgot to mention this earlier. Before Sneaky disappeared when I was having breakfast, he mentioned that I should get some blank tapes so that I could make some recordings of various things that he was going to teach me about Love and the different things a person can do with Love. I assumed that it was going to be some sort of visualization exercise. I was sitting in my chair trying to figure out how to straighten out the problem with the bets when an idea hit me. The more I thought about it the better it seemed and the more I liked it. What I decided to do was make a visualization tape guiding me through a journey into the future. I figured that this would help my mind focus on what I want to achieve, and at the same time take the pressure off. I thought about it all night and worked out the details, writing out every step of the journey. The next morning I got up early and headed to the library to rent a sound effects tape, because I decided to make this as real as possible. I finally got it finished somewhere around two or three in the afternoon. Rudy was pacing around so I decided to take him for a walk before I tried it out. It's a lot easier to relax after you've taken a walk or done some kind of exercise."

"What exactly did you put on the tape?" Danny asked.

"Pretty simple. First I put some music on the beginning of the tape for about five minutes. That was just to relax. Then I would record the visualization that I was standing at a train station waiting for the train. I described what the train station looked like. I also added some sounds that you would hear if you were at a train station, like people talking, footsteps, and so on. Then the train would arrive, and I had the sound effect of a train coming into the station and stopping. This was my own private train and as I boarded the train and sat down, the conductor would come and ask me where I want to go. I would tell the conductor that I wanted to go into the future one-day, and stop at the corner store so I could get off and get a newspaper. I had all the sounds in place so as the train left the station and picked up speed you could hear it, and also the sound of the train traveling. I even used a cup to make my voice sound like the train conductor. The train would travel for about ten minutes, then come to a stop. I would get out of the train, and then I would go to the newspaper stand and pick up tomorrow's paper. Then I would get back on the train, and on the 10-minute trip back to the present, I would read the paper to see the results of the games. The whole thing was approximately 35 minutes long. I figured this would be a lot more fun than trying to focus and meditate for two to three hours at a time."

"Did this work?" Danny looked up from his notes.

"We're getting to that. After Rudy and I got back from our walk in the park, I went into the bedroom to try out my new tape. I had put some earphones into those earmuffs that I was using to keep out the noise. I turned the tape down very low so I could just barely hear the words and the sounds so that I wouldn't be distracted.

Everything was working perfectly. I got on the train and traveled into the future. When the train stopped I got off, purchased a newspaper, and brought it back on the train. I sat down, flipped the paper to the sports section and started reading the results. It wasn't perfect. Everything was a little bit hazy, but I still could make out some results. I was fine with that because I figured it would get better after I practiced it a few times. While I was looking at the results and waiting for the train to leave, I heard the conductor yell, "Coming aboard." I thought, 'wait a minute that's not what I put on the tape. He should have said all aboard.' Then I heard what sounded like footsteps. 'What the heck is going on here?' I wondered. Then I saw him, walking up to where I was sitting. He sat himself down across from me, smirking a very mischievous smirk."

"Hey! This is my private train. What the hell are you doing here?" I said. I tried to erase him from the scene but my imagination was not cooperating. He was really starting to irritate me."

"'Trying to erase your guest? That's not exactly very loving! You sure do have a real attitude problem,' he said."

"'This is too weird,' I said. 'How can you see me? How can I see you? This is not supposed to be real! What do you want?' I could actually feel my heart beating faster."

"'To answer the first question, you're in a heightened state of awareness, and in this state your imagination is a lot more real than you think. Actually you are a lot closer to the real you than you normally are in what you call your physical reality. As for the second question, we are going on a little trip where you will be able to see things as they are and even the way you want to make them.'"

"'You know, my life was going just fine until you showed up,' I responded. 'What do you mean by 'the way I want to make things?''"

"'Nothing has begun,' he said, 'and nothing is finished. But I'll explain that later. In the state that you're in now, you can do things and see things that normally would seem impossible.'"

"I figured I'd play along, thinking that this information might turn out to be useful."

"'So what exactly can I do in this so-called state?' I asked."

"You are in a state of awareness where you are connecting with that larger part of yourself. This part is not limited by your conscious thoughts of what you can or cannot do. You can use your imagination to link to your greater self and its abilities to do anything you want, and create the life you want. Once you understand the process, you'll be able to do it even in your normal awake state.'"

"I could feel and hear the train slowing down. It was just about to stop when Sneaky said, 'Demonstration will commence now. Get off the train now!'"

"The second he said that, I was already standing outside the train. I wasn't at home; I was standing by a very small pond. I recognized it immediately. When I was little, this pond was huge, or at least that's the way I saw it then. This was one of my favorite places. Hardly anyone ever went there. Some people had told me that it was haunted and a monster was supposed to live there. No other kids would ever go there, even when they were chasing me. I was always safe there. This is also the place I first met Sneaky, or at least that's the way I remembered it now."

I looked at Neena and Danny. "Remember that phrase: 'that's the way I remember it now.' This is really important as far as the rest of the story is concerned."

Puzzled, they nodded their heads in agreement.

"I was standing there reminiscing about all the sword fights Sneaky and I had there. Then I saw a small child approaching, wildly swinging a stick like a sword. Holy cow, I thought, that's me! I'm so small! For some reason I didn't think I had ever been that small. I saw myself jumping around swinging a stick sword at one tree after another, so full of life. He walked right up to me, pointed his stick at me, and said, 'So where have you been? I've been looking for you all day.'"

"I didn't know how to react or what to say. I just stood there staring. Everything about him spelled trouble and yet he seemed to be glowing. Just then I heard Sneaky say, 'He sees you as you see me. Have fun.'"

"'Why are you standing there like an idiot? Surrender or fight, you coward!' he said, waving that irritating stick in my face."

"'If you're looking for a battle, then you've found one,' I said, turning to avoid his daring slashes. I broke a branch off a nearby tree and the battle was on. We fought around trees, over rocks, behind bushes, and after who knows how much time we finally settled down on some rocks. I was not even sure exactly where we had ended up but it didn't matter. All that mattered was being alive and having fun."

"He looked at me. 'Why are people so stupid?'"

"'Are they calling you stupid again?' I asked."

"'Yeah,' he said, looking a lot sadder."

"I was thinking about what to say when my lips started to move. It was like I was talking and listening to myself at the same time."

"'They're not really stupid. They just act like that because they're scared.'"

"'Scared of what?'"

"'They're scared of everything; scared of not being loved, scared of too much Love, scared of dying, of living, of not having enough food, scared that others will hurt them or take what they have.' The words were just coming out of my mouth and I was listening to them the same way as he was. 'They're even scared of what they don't have, that others are better than them, of being alone, of being with people, of being made fun of, of not being liked or accepted, scared that something will go wrong, and sometimes they're scared even when things go right. They're scared of those who are not so scared, and most of all, scared of each other.'"

"'So?' he asked with a puzzled look on his face."

"'Fear can drive you to do very unloving things. It can even drive people crazy. It slowly drains all the Love out of life and leaves you with anger that can turn into hate. It all comes down to a lack of Love. Love is the food of the universe and everything in it. Without Love there's chaos, hate, anger, and fear. Where there is Love there is peace, joy, fulfillment, trust, and abundance. That's why things are the way they are, it's just a matter of not being enough Love.'"

"'Where is all this Love then, and why does no one know how to have fun?'"

"'They know how to have fun, they're just afraid and don't trust that they can have fun and survive at the same time. They believe work has to be hard and competitive in a win/lose situation. As far as Love is concerned, it's inside you and everyone, waiting to be released.'"

"'They think they know everything, don't they? They should play and have fun like we do, then everybody would be happy.'"

"'They've forgotten true Love, and some day you'll forget too.'"

I looked at Neena and Danny. "The weird part is that I remember having this conversation with Sneaky when I was little, yet at the same time I know I was having the conversation with myself, only this time I'm the angel. And if that doesn't bend your mind as far as the reality of time is concerned then I don't know what will."

They nodded their heads in agreement.

"He jumped up and started swinging his stick wildly in the air, yelling. 'No, never! No matter what they do, I will fight!'"

"I was just about to say, 'The more you fight it, the more you'll become it,' but I'm not sure if the words left my lips because with a real jolt I found myself back in my bedroom. Dazed and still in shock, I could hear someone calling my name. It was my friend Jeff. I could hear him in the kitchen. I got up and met him halfway down the hallway, I was still half out of it and rubbing my eyes."

"'What the heck are you doing, sleeping again?' he asked."

"'Yeah, just having a nap.'"

"'In the middle in the day, he's sleeping.' Jeff shook his head as he walked into the living room and planted himself on the couch."

"'I was working on the odds and fell asleep. Then I had a weird dream. I see you brought beer.' I sat down, still trying to orient myself.'"

"'I'll put it in the fridge.' He took the beer into the kitchen. 'You look like shit. You look like you've seen a ghost.'"

"He walked back into the living room and handed me a beer. 'You're losing it, buddy. You'd better stop this time travel stuff.' I just laughed with him, thinking 'if you only knew!'"

"'You keep doing this mind stuff and you'll end up calling out horse races from a nice warm padded room, and you'll have it all to yourself.'" He laughed.

"'Yeah, and you'll be putting money on them!'"

"'As long as you're right. I'll bring you some cigarettes every couple of days.'"

"'What about my share of the winnings?'"

"'Oh, I'll hang onto them for you, no problem,' he smirked."

"We spent the next four or five hours drinking and arguing whether it is possible to predict the future. His argument was that the future has not been played out yet and so is unpredictable. My argument is that the future, the present, and the past are one and time is an illusion; therefore the future not only can be calculated and predicted, but also can be created. If he weren't so stubborn and thickheaded, he'd be able to see that. Of course he thinks I'm the thickheaded one. He says I'm just lucky. I say there is no such a thing as luck. He thinks the universe is random. I say there is nothing random in the universe. He thinks I'm full of shit. Well guess what I think. And on it goes, as long as there are players, the game plays."

Details

A thousand variations
Even so it is said
There are only two types of actions
An action of Love
Or
A cry for more Love
But variations
There will be a thousand

Chapter Twenty-Three

I pulled my last cigarette out of my last pack. "You'd better have some cig-arettes behind the counter or this story is over, which is too bad because it's just getting good."

"I don't have any," Danny said as I lit my cigarette.

Neena opened her purse, which was lying on the bar by her left hand. I watched her reach into her purse with her right hand and pull out a brand new package of cigarettes. As she set them in front of me I saw that they were my brand.

Danny lifted his eyebrow.

"Now there's my kind of woman: soft, tough, caring, mysterious and most of all handy," I said.

"Danny, you might want to make some notes from here on because what you're going to learn from the rest of the story is going to make you forget all about the lottery. Are you single?"

He gave me a very puzzled look. "Yes."

"You're not going to be single for very much longer. Scared yet?"

"What if I don't make any notes?" he asked.

"Suit yourself," I answered, "just remember I did warn you because I'm not going to repeat it."

"The next day I ran some errands and went to the library to pick up some books and tapes on Love. I wanted to see if I could find anything on sending Love. In some ways this was starting to get exciting mostly because I now was sure that I could keep on winning and not have to go back to work at something that I didn't want to do. I didn't dislike work; it just never seemed very satisfying or fulfilling to me. I really felt alive and felt that I had my whole life still head of me to discover what would bring me joy. By the time evening came I had listened to a few tapes and read a little. I started to think about the train ride that I had the day before. I remembered the scene from my childhood very clearly now. I remembered Sneaky telling me that I would end up becoming everything that I hated in everyone else. I also remembered him telling me that I would forget him and everything he had shown me and that I would spend a large part of my life looking for Love on the outside and would forget that Love comes from the inside. He had also told me that I would experience life with very little Love and that someday this would be a very valuable lesson. In some way it all made sense, but at the same time that I didn't have a lot of answers, I did have of questions. I decided to write down all my questions so that *I* could drill Sneaky when he came back. I wrote about three pages and the more I wrote the more I realized that I did not have a clue about what was going on. By 11 PM, I was exhausted and dragged myself to bed."

I stopped for a moment to open the new package of cigarettes that Neena gave me.

"So what am I supposed to write in my notes?" asked Danny, holding his pen.

"Just the stuff that is associated with sending Love which we'll get back to in a bit."

"Relax, Danny. Let him tell the story the way it happened." Neena chuckled.

"The next morning I woke up in the middle of a dream. I was dreaming that a clown was shaking my bed, and when I opened my eyes, Sneaky was standing at the end of the bed. I sheepishly looked at my watch. It said 11:30. I looked at Sneaky and asked if he had woke me up."

"'I just thought I would let you know that Rudy just ran out of his doggy door chasing a cat.'"

"I turned over and closed my eyes to go back to sleep. I was just about to doze off again when I heard Sneaky say, 'He didn't stop at the fence. He's running down the road at this very minute.'"

"I jumped out of bed and started putting on my clothes. 'Oh, man, why didn't you stop him? I can't afford the two hundred dollars for his bail if he gets caught.'"

"'You could call him back with Love instead of running around looking for him,' Sneaky said."

"'Why don't you just tell me where he is?' I was starting to get a little grumpy."

"'Why don't you just send Love and see what happens? Besides, I'm not your guardian angel. It's not my job.'"

"'For an angel, you have a real attitude problem. And if you're not my guardian angel, then what the hell are you?'"

"'Aren't we cranky in the mornings?'"

"'Are you going to help me or not?'"

"'Why don't you use your train visualization to go see him and ask him to come home? Don't forget to send Love.'"

"I stopped for a moment to clear my thoughts. 'Are you sure this is going to work?' I pointed my finger at him. 'This had better not be part of your twisted sense of humor.'"

"'Just try it. What do you have to lose? I'll walk you through it. It's as easy as breathing.'"

I walked into the living room and lay down on the couch, thinking to myself that this had better work.

"'OK, I'm ready,' I said, 'but if he's not back in 15 minutes, I'm going after him.'"

"I listened to his instructions and followed them exactly. Somewhere along the line I must have fallen asleep again because when I woke up Rudy was standing there licking my face and wagging his tail. I'm not sure how long it was until he came home, but nevertheless it worked. During the time I was following Sneaky's instructions, I told Rudy that if he came home I would take him for a walk. So I had some breakfast and then took a shower and shortly after took Rudy for a walk."

"While Rudy was playing with the other dogs at the park I thought about Love and where this Love comes from. If it is coming from me, why would Sneaky say that I was starving for Love in the past and that this lack of Love was causing me all this inner pain? The more I thought about it the more confusing it became. The only conclusion I came up with was that perhaps there is a massive amount of Love inside all of us, but it's in a little sealed package that we need to open to release it. In some ways that made sense. While I was thinking about all of this I suddenly realized that I wasn't feeling sad or any inner pain anymore. And that's why lately I've felt so at peace even though financially I should be a nervous wreck. I'm not that sure exactly when this change came about. It's like having migraine headaches forever and then one day they're gone. You get so used to having them that perhaps you don't see when they slip away. I came to the conclusion that maybe I didn't notice the change because there was so much going on lately. The other thing I thought about in the park was that Sneaky had said he wasn't my guardian angel. So the question is, what is he? Every time I see him or think about him my instincts keep saying there's something not quite right. I couldn't put my finger on it. But I knew I wasn't seeing things as they really are."

"So the only question that remains right now is, do you want the instructions, Danny?" I waited for his reply.

Neena nodded.

Danny shrugged. "I don't have a dog."

"That's not the point. You can use this for a lot of different things. Perhaps someday you might be looking for someone. Perhaps someday you might be looking for your son or daughter. Or you might have a disagreement with someone and you can use this to go and speak with them and work it out.

The things you can do with this are endless. All you need to do is use your imagination. I even found some lost objects using this method."

Danny sat there thinking. Neena said, "How about the next time you're looking for a job? You could use this to meet the person who is going to interview you."

"I've done that," I answered, "and it works like a charm. The minute you walk into the interview it will feel like you've met before. And surprisingly, the other person feels the same way. There is a catch, though. Everything you say when you meet this person in this mind state must be totally honest, because you can lie with your lips but not with your mind. If you are not telling the truth it will always be noticed, and that will backfire on you. Been there, done that, didn't work."

"There's one other little catch. Somebody I know used it to visit her lover who was out of the country. Unfortunately she was so positive that he might be cheating that after she visited him a couple of times, she actually saw him with someone. Immediately afterwards, she phoned him at work and was able to reach him on the construction site. As it turned out, it wasn't true. You need to let go of what you're going to see so that you are not using your imagination to create something that is not there. After that everything went so smoothly that he phoned her a few times shortly after she had visited him to tell her that he could feel her presence. In the end it became quite a game with them, and from what she has told me it has brought them closer together and created a inner bond that wasn't there before, even though much of their time is spent apart. So do you want it or not? Make up your mind, I haven't got all night."

"So why don't you ask me if I want to hear the instructions?" asked Neena with a big grin.

"Because you already know how to do it, and I've figured this little game out, so let's just keep playing." I answered feeling a little proud of myself.

"If that's the case, give the instructions and let's get on with the story, shall we?"

"Anyway, the important thing is to find a quiet place and make yourself really comfortable. Try to get some of those construction earmuffs so that you're not disturbed by any noise. Breathe deeply and slowly and bring yourself into a deep state of relaxation. Give yourself some time to do this. And at the same time bring your focus and attention to listening to your inner self, or soul, or God, whatever you want to choose for yourself. I still believe that this is the fastest way of getting the mind to become quiet, because you are putting all your attention into listening for something that you can only barely hear. When you feel you are ready, imagine yourself becoming lighter, and by becoming lighter and lighter you are raising your vibration. Sort of like musical notes going higher and higher. Put a bubble of light around yourself as if you are in a balloon and begin to float upwards. As you do this, imagine that you are floating to wherever you want to go. This will only take a few seconds. Time and distance means nothing to the mind or your consciousness. Don't allow yourself to see whatever or whoever it is you want to see. Don't concern yourself with the surroundings unless that is important to you. It's important to send Love and surround and fill whoever or whatever you are visiting with Love. You may want to surround yourself with Love also. Now if you want to communicate with them, do so, but in a very loving manner. Be sure to listen. You may or may not hear actual words, but you may get impressions in your thoughts of what this other person may be telling you. Be honest…tell it like it is. Whatever you do, do it from your heart, not from your ego. If you've made promises, stick to them. When you're done, slowly bring yourself back. Before getting up, take time to think about what you said or heard."

"For instance, if you consciously talk to someone, they may not know it, and there is a good chance they will not, but you are talking to a part of them and in some way their subconscious will make every effort possible to relay this information to their conscious mind. This may come for them in the senses or feelings or intuition. You do not need to be afraid of interfering with someone's privacy because at every stage of each person's development, those areas will be dealt with and handled by the larger part of each person involved, depending on the relationship you have with this person. Have fun, share Love."

"This exercise will take at least twenty minutes. At first it will most likely take longer because of the extra time needed to become totally relaxed. By relaxed I mean that your body should be asleep to the point where you can't feel it any more. That is when you will probably get the best results."

"Later on, after you have had some experience with this you can change the method and perhaps use an imaginary train to get where you want to go. But at first I suggest that you use the bubble of light instead so that you are not engaging too much of your imagination."

"And remember you're not always right. No one ever is."

"So is that it?" Danny asked.

"Yea, when pigs fly."

Relationships

Relationships are sort of
Like grabbing a bull
By the horns
But if there's Love, trust, and intimacy
From both sides,
You might just come to see
Eye to eye.
Oh, all the snorting
And head spinning...
I hate that when that happens.
The things you gotta do
For a kiss on the lips.

Chapter Twenty-Four

"Let's get back to the rest of the story," I said. "On the way home from the park, Rudy and I stopped at the store to purchase some cigarettes and the sports odds for that day. On the way back to the house I thought about my financial situation. I had enough money to buy groceries, gas and cigarettes but not really enough to pay the bills. No matter how good I felt, I thought if I didn't get all those bills caught up, sooner or later the shit was going to hit the fan."

"When we got home I decided to make a small change on my visualization tape with the train ride. I decided that after taking the train to the future and reading the paper that I would just continue with the train and see where it would take me. Most of the bets didn't need to be in until six or seven that night which gave me plenty of time. After changing the tape, I had a little snack and headed for the bedroom. Everything went smoothly and perfectly. I got off my imaginary train, picked up the paper, got back on the train, and opened the paper to read the results while waiting for the train to continue. I could see the results of the games perfectly. It was amazing. I could read the entire paper as if I had just bought it in reality. I heard the conductor yell 'all aboard' and felt the train begin to move. I was quite excited by how things were turning out. Then I noticed that the train seemed to be going faster and faster. I looked to see where the conductor was, but couldn't see him. I tried to slow the train down but it wouldn't. I thought this was weird, this is my imagination, so I should be able to control this. Then it hit me: Sneaky is at it again! Suddenly the train made a dead stop. The conductor walked past and said 'We have arrived.' As I got off the train I found myself standing in what seemed like a courtyard, like a temple. It was very beautiful. Everything seemed to be made of crystals or pure light. Everything definitely seemed to glow with light. I couldn't see a sun, but there was an incredible amount of very bright but not blinding light. At the same time everything seemed to be a little bit hazy. I wasn't sure whether the light caused this or if I wasn't seeing correctly. It was a lot like dreaming, but the best way I can describe it is that I was totally aware and consciously awake. As I stood there I realized the place was filled with Love. It was so thick with Love that I could feel Love flowing into my lungs as I breathed. I could touch it, feel it, sense it; it was incredible. It was like someone dunked me in liquid Love. I never felt anything like this before. I was stuffing this Love into my body, and don't even bother asking me to explain that. I just kept shoving it down into my body and filling myself more and more. I was so totally absorbed in trying to get all the Love I could that I didn't notice when the beings had appeared in front of me. I looked at them and for a split second felt a little guilty for being such a pig. But their response was to send me more Love. I felt totally, absolutely and unquestionably loved by them. I couldn't see them very clearly, but I came to the conclusion that one of the three of them was Sneaky. Then I noticed there seemed to be one more standing behind the three. I got the impression that they were shielding me from the being that was behind them because he seemed to be glowing so brightly that he was almost on fire. I looked towards the being that I thought was Sneaky and in that same moment I saw Sneaky's face. Instantly another being moved directly in front of me and took what appeared to be a sword and stuck it into the top of my head and shoved it down to the bottom of my spine. There was no pain, and it all happened so fast that I just stood there. As soon as he had pushed the sword in he pulled another and shoved it into my forehead, sending it out the back of my head, then another through my temples and another into the center of my chest. I felt like I was opening and more Love was flowing in. Maybe because of that

I didn't react. I just felt that everything was OK. Then I noticed that they were not swords at all, but seemed to be rods of light. I was just standing there letting the Love pour into me. The next thing I remember was being back in my room. The first thing I did was write down the bets that I wanted to make. Looking at the clock, I realized I only had ten minutes to get those bets in, so I headed straight for the store."

"When I watched the results of the games later that night, I saw that I had won enough to tie me over for at least a couple more weeks. But somehow it wasn't important because I felt so good."

I stopped for a moment. "I could sit here for the next two hours and try it to describe how fantastic I felt, but there are no words to describe the feeling of being filled with Love. I wouldn't even know where to begin."

"Wow! So how do I get there?" Danny asked.

"That's not the point. I'm going to show you how to do that yourself, there's a whole universe of Love locked up in a little tiny box in each of us and all we need to do is open it. This must be one of the best-kept secrets. It's almost like humanity has been steered away from actually finding this. I don't know who or what is responsible for hiding this ability we have, which should be ours to use and share. Have you ever noticed when you watch a scary movie that in some manner or another, they're always trying to convince you that Love has very little power? That's so ridiculous that it's not even funny. That's like telling somebody that the firecracker you are holding is only going to make a little noise. Just let me finish telling the rest of the story and you'll see what I mean."

Neena started rubbing my back. "How about making us some tea Danny Klaus is getting a little worked up."

"Is it that obvious? Actually, some tea would be quite nice."

They say that the best way to a man's heart is through the stomach, which is fairly true, but in my case a nice back rub works about ten times as fast.

Inner Love

Inner Love is a
Natural experience
But when we cover
It with fear,
Anger, mistrust, and shame
We search for it in
Others

Chapter Twenty-Five

"It was at least a week before Sneaky came back. During that week I made several bets and took several train rides. I was having reasonably good results even though not as good as when I first started with all of this. But it was enough to put some money into my pocket and get me by for a little longer. I was also offered a job out of the blue, which I decided to turn down. It is hard to say whether I made the best decision. I didn't want to work at something that I would not enjoy doing just to survive. That's a very fast way to turn life into a grueling experience. Besides there's no point in grabbing the bull by the horns if you don't want to be thrown around a little. On top of that I was feeling so fantastic for the first time in my life that I was not going to screw it up for anything. As the week started to wind down I noticed that the amount of Love seemed to be diminishing. Perhaps it was being used up. I had made several attempts to return to this temple, but each time I would end up somewhere else. By the end of the week I was back to how I felt before. There was no doubt about it, I was definitely running out of Love."

"I was just returning from one of my train trips when I opened my eyes, Sneaky was standing at the end of my bed."

"'Hey, it's about time you showed up!' I sat up in my bed."

"'Running out of Love, are we?' he asked."

"'Let's go back there!'"

"'Not so fast!' he grinned, 'it's up to you to give yourself that Love.'"

"'Why can't I get anymore from there? Wherever there is.'"

"You can, but it's better that you learn that the Love you now want lies inside you and all you need to do is learn to open the valve.'"

"'What do you mean? I don't get it.'"

"'When you fall in Love, you begin to radiate with Love, and you get all the feelings that go with it. But in fact the Love comes from inside you, from the being that you truly are. In a sense, you are using falling in Love with someone as a trigger mechanism to open your heart to the Love that is inside you. It is possible to fall in Love with someone who is not in Love with you and still feel all the Love, because actually the Love comes from inside of you. Just because you may not be in Love with one particular person at this present time, it doesn't mean that you cannot have Love and feel Love and be surrounded with Love. The reason you can send Love to your food or another person or the environment or whatever it may be is because there is an endless and infinite supply of Love in you waiting to be opened. We thought that it might be best to give you a demonstration to show you what is possible."

"I took a few minutes to think about it. There's no doubt in my mind that I was suckered, hook, line, and sinker, but what choice did I have? I just had one of the best weeks of my life and I wasn't going to let it slide by."

"So are you going to show me how or are you going to just stand there and blabber about it?"

"Glad to have you aboard again." Sneaky grinned from ear to ear. "You might want to get a blank tape and record this for yourself. It will work the first time, but if you want to have as much as you had last week it will take a little practice."

"I don't know why I ended up with an angel who has a rotten sense of humor. I got my tape recorder and a blank tape and we made the recording. Sneaky told me what to say, then I recorded it onto the tape. After the tape was finished Sneaky disappeared again. I didn't bother trying it out that day but the next morning I cashed in some winning tickets and picked up some groceries. It looked like the weather was going to turn cold."

"From here on, it's not easy to explain in words everything that happened, and everything may not be totally in the right order, but I'm sure you'll get the drift."

"I tried listening to the tape twice, but I stopped using it because it was so easy to do that I felt I didn't need the tape. I got results the very first time, but not what I had felt on that particular week. I figured if a little bit is good then a whole lot must be better; maybe all I needed was a little more practice. I decided to give it all I had. And that's exactly what I did for the next nine days. Opening my heart and radiating Love is basically all I did. I would spend an hour doing it then I would take a break for perhaps one hour and then do it again. This is something that you may want to think about before you do it to that extent. It's best to start off slowly. That way you will get used to the things that are going to transpire. Love is very addictive, and the better I felt, the more I did it. I wanted to see if there really was a limit on how much Love a person could feel. It just never occurred to me that it would affect everything and everyone around me."

"The first few days were fairly cold, so I spent all my time indoors filling myself with Love and radiating it out. During those first few days I didn't take Rudy for his daily walks because of the weather. I was feeling really great and at peace. There was a deep inner joy that seemed to flow to the surface. Even though I was alone and had no company during this time I was not lonely. I felt very loved and more connected to the world, yet at the same time unaffected by what seems to go on in the world. The more Love I filled myself with, the more these feelings increased. Any emotional pain from the past seemed to just slip away. I'm hardly doing it justice, but unfortunately I just don't have the words to describe something so beautiful." I shrugged my shoulders.

"After a few days the weather warmed up and I started taking Rudy for his daily walks. That's when I noticed things were different. At first I couldn't really put my finger on it because there were so many little things that were slightly different. Everything seemed brighter, more alive, and more colorful. The air seemed to be full of life. During the first few days there weren't many people in the park walking their dogs, so what started to happen didn't really sink in until a few days later. At first I noticed that there seemed to be birds following us wherever we walked. Not a lot of birds, just a few. Another thing I noticed is that as soon as other people's dogs saw me, they would run towards me and literally try to jump on me. This doesn't sound strange except that most of the dogs are usually interested in playing with the other dogs and don't pay much attention to the humans in the park. Also I noticed that people began to be extremely friendly, much more than they normally were, almost in a flirtatious way. It wasn't as bad as the time in the supermarket the day after I first met Sneaky, but it was slowly getting like that. In some way I saw what was coming and in another way I didn't believe it. So I decided to just keep going and see what happened. As the days went by it got more bizarre each day. Women started flirting with me aggressively, in some cases even using their bodies. It's like the walls came down and personal space became nonexistent. Even men were acting strange, almost like we were buddies for a very long time. If I stopped and talked to someone, other people would join in, which isn't all that bizarre by it's self except that everyone's attention seemed to be focused on me. People seemed to do a lot of physical touching while they were talking to me. Let's face it: people in a city do not touch strangers in the park. There is usually a certain distance that is maintained by everyone."

Danny looked at me in disbelief.

"You don't have to believe anything I tell you, Danny, but there is no reason for me to lie. You can experience this yourself very easily if you want to. It gets even more bizarre. A friend of mine asked me to go for a drink with him after he got off work. We decided to meet at a certain bar. I managed to get there about twenty minutes before him. The bar where we were going to meet is fairly large and it was happy hour. There were a lot of people there. I walked in looked around and didn't see him. I found myself an open spot at the bar and ordered a drink. While I was waiting, I decided that I might as well continue to fill myself with Love and radiate it out. Within fifteen minutes women started to migrate to where I was sitting. I decided to stand and gave my chair to one of the women that was standing very close. By the time my friend came into the bar I was totally surrounded with women. I'm telling you the truth. They were packed around me like we were in a crowded bus. If they had all known each other, I could have told myself that I was just standing at the right place at the right time, but that wasn't the case. When I saw my friend coming I managed to squeeze myself out of that very tight situation and we went to the other side of the bar. He had seen where I came from and made some comments about why I didn't stay there. We spent the next few minutes talking and joking back and forth. Within a few minutes we were surrounded with women. My friend was having a pretty good time and when I finally decided it was time for me to get out of there, he was too busy to even consider objecting to my leaving so early. I'm a very quiet person and prefer to be in small groups. I wasn't used to having that much attention and some of these women really seemed to mean business. On the way home I decided to stop at the grocery store and pick up a few things, and that turned out to be a repeat of the first time. I was very happy to get home and sit in my favorite chair without being mauled. I was thinking to myself that there was no way I could go through life like that. That twit of an angel should have told me that there would be side effects."

"Then I heard a voice. 'Side effects?'"

"As I turned my head I saw Sneaky sitting on the sofa."

"Yeah, side effects," I said. "People were downright friendly. You should have told me there were risks involved."

"That must have been all he could take because he broke out in laughter and laughed so hard he disappeared."

"I guess it was pretty funny, although I wasn't laughing at the time. About an hour later Sneaky came back and took one look at me. He smiled and I thought I heard some laughing just as he disappeared again. Later that evening I decided for some strange reason to organize all my bills and stack them in a nice little pile. This is not one of my normal activities so I assumed that this idea came from Sneaky. By the time I was ready for bed they were all sorted into a stack about four inches high."

I took a sip of my tea and excused myself to go to the washroom.

What to do?

What do you want to do right now?
Would it bring
You and me
More Love and joy?
Then forget the rest!

Chapter Twenty-Six

As I came out of the washroom, I saw that the old man who has been sitting at the table was gone. I was trying to remember if I saw him sitting there when I went into the washroom but I wasn't sure. Walking back to my chair, I decided that the game was coming to an end. Maybe I should have asked where he went and who he was, but I didn't think I would get a straight answer so I decided to leave it alone.

I took a sip of tea. "OK, where was I?"

Danny asked for the instructions for how to surround himself with Love.

"I'll give you the instructions in a minute," I answered. "But first let me tell you how to use it and how it was explained to me, so that you won't get yourself into too much trouble. Otherwise Neena is going to have to be your bodyguard."

"I'm just going to stand back and watch Danny squirm." Neena laughed.

"Over the next couple of days I stopped working with Love and went back to focusing on my bets. It wasn't going that well even though I was still making some money. It just seemed like there was something stopping me."

"A few days after Sneaky's visit, he showed up one morning shortly after I had breakfast. I had been waiting for him to show up and as soon as I saw him I asked, 'Why didn't you tell me that I was going to turn into some kind of people, bird, and dog magnet?'"

"'I decided to let you see for yourself the power of Love. You wouldn't have believed me if you hadn't experienced it for yourself.'"

"'What's the point in that? I can't even go to the store.'"

"'Oh, it's not that bad. Working with Love is an art. It's all in how you do it.'"

"'I did it exactly the way you told me to do it.'"

"Let me explain it to you this way. There isn't enough Love in the world and people are desperately looking for it, so when you begin to radiate with Love, a small imbalance is created. If everyone knew and understood how to open their hearts then you would not see the same results, or some of the actions that you observed. People would still be drawn to each other and animals would be drawn towards people, but it would not be focused on one individual in a room. Do you understand what I'm saying?"

"'Sure, that makes sense, but it doesn't solve my problem of what I'm going to do in the meantime, because I don't see the rest of the world doing this in the very near future.'"

"'You are going to be pleasantly surprised in a very short time. You'll get used to the attention, and after a while it won't bother you anymore because you're going to like It.'" he said. 'All you need to do is make some changes in the way you radiate Love. It's just a matter of getting you to stop whining long enough so that I can explain it.'"

"I was going to defend myself, but he had a point. So I sat there and listened."

"There are many ways you can work with Love. When you open your heart and radiate Love, you become like a very small sun. Even though other people cannot consciously see this Love they can feel it, and subconsciously they know exactly what's happening. Your subconscious will send your conscious mind messages to go towards the person who is radiating with Love. The subconscious can communicate this to the conscious mind in many ways, like impulses to do something, an attraction for the person radiating with Love and so on. Another way for you to play with Love is when you go to a meeting or to someone's house where other people will be, you can send Love, filling the room with Love before you even get there. You can do this for a business meeting, party, family get together, or a job interview. Can you imagine what would happen if you had a business that was filled with Love and all the employees were radiant with Love?'"

"I nodded. 'It would probably attract a lot of customers.'"

"'You can also send Love directly to people in different ways, which will have slightly different results. You can send Love to other people and surround them with Love, like draping them in a warm blanket of Love. Or you can fill them with Love. You can also send Love directly to their heart area. This will do many different things depending on the person. This will help another individual to actually open their own heart, for as Love enters their heart area, you will most likely find that they will begin to glow with Love themselves. This works very well if you want to be closely connected with someone, perhaps a mate or your children. We'll be discussing this more later.'"

"'It's starting to get more and more complicated." I didn't know what else to say."

"'Not at all. Think of a person right now who you feel needs more Love.'"

"'If you put it that way, we're talking about everybody in the world, Sneaky!'"

He gave me a look.

"'OK, I'm thinking of someone. Now what?'"

"'Just decide which method would be the best way at this very moment to send Love to this person. You can fill their home with Love, send Love to their workplace, surround them with Love, fill them with Love, or send Love to their heart center. Take whatever comes to your mind and feels right for the moment. Sometimes even two or three different ways will be perfect.'"

"'That's actually pretty easy. Their home is a war zone, so filling their home with Love would probably help them work things out, or at least prevent killing each other in the process. Am I right?'"

"'Perfect.'"

I looked out the window for a minute while I thought about it. When I looked back, he had disappeared again.

Danny was making a few notes so I stopped for a moment to let him catch up.

"So is filling yourself and sending Love something like when you fall in Love?" Neena asked.

"It's exactly like that. You feel the same things. You feel good all over. When two people fall in Love they seem to glow. There's something different about them and you've probably noticed how they also tend to attract people. Men have said this to me often, that when they're with someone in a relationship there seems to be women everywhere, yet if they're not in a relationship, attracting women seems to be more difficult."

"That all makes perfect sense now," Danny said. "Every time I'm with someone and we're feeling really good about each other, I seem to attract women and people in general. I can't believe it, it's so simple and the answer has been right there in front of us, and nobody caught it. It makes so much sense I can't imagine how we could possibly have missed it."

"There's a reason why this information seems to have eluded everyone for centuries, and the answer is pretty scary, but we won't get into that right now because it's not going to make any difference anymore. Once people know how to work with Love and they see the results, it's going to be impossible to stop."

Danny's eyes opened wide. "Are you telling me that something or someone has kept this information from everyone? Why?"

"Love is the most powerful force anywhere, and we have an endless supply of Love. That means we are not helpless little creatures. The nice thing about Love is that it actually has its own consciousness. You can only do positive things with Love. When we send Love to another person, the Love will affect that person in whatever way is best for them, no matter what you do. Sending Love to another person is only the beginning of what you can do with it! The best way to say it is that there is nothing that you can't do with Love. As far as pointing a finger to what is responsible for hiding this knowledge the bottom line is that we allowed them to do this so in the end it is we who are responsible. Working with Love, playing with Love, is something that a child should be taught from the minute they can speak. That's the best gift anyone could possibly give."

"Can I have the instructions now?" Danny smiled.

"My pleasure."

Dreams

Hell is watching your
Dreams die.
Because it's not just your
Dream that dies.
So we might as well
Die chasing our dreams
That way, at least, we have
Lived for something.

Chapter Twenty-Seven

After I finished giving Danny the instructions on how to fill himself with Love and send Love out, I gave him a few minutes to finish making his notes.

"It was probably four or five days before Sneaky came back. By then I had made changes in how I was playing with Love. This made all the difference. People still seemed to be attracted to me, or perhaps I should say I was still magnetic to people, but not to the extent it was before. It was at a level that I could handle, and I started using humor to create a distance and to better handle the people that were coming my direction. This turned out to work very well for me. I also realized that I could turn it off at any time, which for some reason had never dawned on me before. When Sneaky came back I was sitting in the living room staring at the stack of bills on my coffee table. It was quite a stack."

"'Wow! That's quite a stack of bills you've collected.' He grinned from ear to ear."

"A thought occurred to me. 'When you disappear and I can't see you anymore, where do you go?'"

"'The future, the past, the present; it's all the same.'"

"'Any chance you could take me with you?' I asked, hinting that I need to get away from these bills."

"'Where I go or how I get there is not the issue. You'll figure that out pretty soon. Right now we need to deal with some other issues, and not only the bills.'"

"'Right now, the only problem I see are these bills, and if you take them with you, the problem is solved.'"

"'I think the main issue right now is that you need to stop running from life and running from things that you don't like or feel that you can't handle, unless, of course, you want to continue the way you've been living. It's your decision.'"

I stopped trying to be a smart-ass for a minute because I knew he was right. I had been running in circles.

"'Have you ever noticed how many things have gone wrong in my life? It's like everything is broken. I don't know what to do with my life. I don't even know anymore what I like to do. I definitely don't want to spend the rest of my life doing something I don't like just to survive. I'm pretty sure that life isn't supposed to be that complicated. Is it?'"

"'I know what you're saying,' he said. 'But I can't change your life for you, because then it would not be your life anymore. But I can show you how to effectively overcome one challenge at a time. Once an issue or a challenge or a problem…whatever you want to call them…is dealt with, they don't come back. But if you keep trying to run from them or ignore them, they just pile up and you'll have more and more to deal with until it feels hopeless. Doesn't this sound familiar?'"

"I was squirming around in my chair because I saw my life as one big pile of something, and I could see how it could easily take twenty years to straighten all this out, which would be just in time for me to kick the bucket."

"Sneaky must have heard my thoughts. 'It's not going to take twenty years.' He was laughing now. "You have no concept of where you'll be in five years, but it shouldn't take you much longer to catch on. There's no point in turning a molehill into a mountain. You just take care of it while it's still a molehill. Any problem can be solved with Love, even the ones in the past.'"

"'Love or no Love, you can't change the past.'"

"'The past is no more finished than the present moment. The past, present, and future are the same. They are only different snapshots taken of split moments, and it doesn't matter what order you play them in. You have seen what Love can do; even though it's only been a very small demonstration, there's more to come. You know you can travel into the future and use that knowledge to win your sports lottery. So why do you think you can't go into the past and send Love there and change everything?'"

"I had to think for a moment because he seemed to have a point, but I wondered how it would affect the present if I went into the past and sent Love to myself. The concept intrigued me."

"'For now let's just deal with these bills. I'll be back in two days, and by then perhaps you will have given the illusion of time some more thought.'"

"'Let me guess, you want me to send Love to these bills. Am I right?' I shook my head."

"'Precisely,' he answered. 'Take one bill at a time and send Love to it, then send Love to the company that you owe this money to, then send Love to all the people who are responsible for collecting this money and looking after the bills.'"

"'I've never met these people, so how am I supposed to send them Love? I don't even know how many there are.'"

"'It doesn't matter. Just use your imagination and send Love until you feel you've reached all the people involved. You'll know when you're done. And to answer your next question, just keep at it until they are paid.'"

"'I guess this means they're not going to disappear on their own?'"

"'Life can feel like a long process, but once you get the hang of it and you've dealt with some of the main challenges, it will be fun and exciting. It won't take very long before you feel you can handle any challenge and change it for the better. You've already started. You needed more Love and now you've learned where this Love comes from and what it can do. In time you will get better and better at it.'"

"'Excuse me, but that's not the question I asked.'"

"'Life is like a school and the courses are Love, understanding, patience, trust and learning to create what you want with Love. So now all you need to do is decide once and for all whether you're going to give it all you've got or hide under a rock.'"

"I had a feeling that he was going to try to disappear without me seeing how he did it, so I continued to stare at him. I wanted to see exactly how he disappeared, whether he just faded away gradually or slipped away all at once. While I was staring at him I noticed something strange. I had to look a certain way at him and squint my eyes a bit, but it almost seemed like he looked like me. A moment later I had no choice but to blink, and in that moment he was gone."

"What happened to the bills?" Danny asked.

"I paid them. I'm not sure how, but eight months later they were all paid. The interesting part was that no one ever called me to collect.

"What about the fact that Sneaky looked like you?" Neena asked.

"That's a good question. I spent quite a few hours trying to put the pieces together, but we'll get to that shortly. Got anymore tea?"

Time

Time is the magician,
That makes the illusion.
Of a billion snapshots,
Look like movement.
Without time
We would be frozen
In the moment.
Which moment?
Every moment.

Chapter Twenty-Eight

"Sneaky came back two days later, just as he had said he would. We didn't talk anymore about the bills. I had done what he suggested and I assumed he knew that. We did get into a discussion about time and reality."

"'Let's get down to the nitty gritty. Why are you stopping me from winning the sports lottery?'"

"Sneaky laughed. 'So you finally had the guts to ask me.'"

"'So you admit it.'"

"'No! No one is stopping you, except you.' He grinned from ear to ear again."

"'Why would I stop myself? That makes no sense.'"

"'You have some conflicting beliefs. At first you believed totally that it was possible, then you began to doubt yourself, and immediately you saw the results of your doubts, which proved to you that your beliefs are correct, which then resulted in more evidence that you were correct. First comes thought, then comes results, positive or negative depending on the thought.'"

"I was trying to think what kind of thoughts or beliefs I had that could have been conflicting with what I wanted to achieve."

"'You believed that this was too good to be true and something would end up interfering with you. The more results you got the more you started to believe that this was too good to be true. Am I right?'"

"I had to agree because he was right, that's exactly what I was thinking, yet at the same time I didn't even realize it."

"'There's one more issue you seem to have forgotten about.'"

"'And that is?'"

"'Which future are you predicting? The future is not written in stone and there are endless probabilities. Past, present, and future are the same. What makes them appear different is time. Time is the magician that takes a snapshot of a single moment and gives them the illusion of movement and of one coming before the other.'"

"'I understand that.'"

"'Not really. If you had fully understood it you would be looking at everything differently. Your life and everything you see and experience are tiny snapshots of reality. There are billions upon billions of them, which you subconsciously sort out in the order that you want them to appear, then time takes them and turns them into a film which you perceive as continuous moments of past, present, and future. When you believe something or have conflicting beliefs, the appropriate snapshots of reality are inserted into the film of your life, which you not only watch but also participate in. That means if you can send Love now, here in the present, to someone, then you can take the snapshot of what you consider the past and send Love to any period of time.'"

"'So how do I figure out which probable future is going to happen as far as the games are concerned?'"

"'Everyone who watches the game, plays in the game, and has a stake in it, in one way or another decides how the game will be played and what the outcome will be. It's simple: the majority rules. Just tell your mind to show you the most predictable, probable future. Unfortunately changes in the probable future can be made minute by minute as the majority changes its mind. As you can see if you are trying to achieve one hundred percent accuracy, you are expending an enormous amount of energy, and that is not worthwhile. You could be using that energy to work with Love and achieve much greater results.'"

"I was about to ask another question when I realized he had already disappeared."

"What he said makes sense," said Danny as he put down my cup of tea. "Except I'm not sure if I understand the snapshot of reality."

"You don't need to totally understand it." Neena said. "What's important is that you understand that each time you have a thought or a belief, a snapshot of reality reflecting that thought or belief will be placed into the film of your life and you will experience it."

"Don't forget the buffer zone." I interjected.

"What's the buffer zone?" Danny asked.

"Not every thought goes into the film, or life would just be totally crazy. So there's a buffer zone. Only the thoughts that are directly connected to the beliefs you have that you are totally certain about will be placed into the film. But if there is a conflicting belief, then either both pictures representing the beliefs, or a combination of the two, or neither, will be inserted, depending on the strength of those beliefs."

"That makes sense," Danny nodded.

As I added some sugar to my tea, Neena decided she also wanted another cup. Personally I thought it had more to do with having Danny serve her. I'm quite sure she enjoyed that more than the tea itself, but then I'm just going by the look on her face.

Patience

Patience has never been
One of my virtues.
The thing is, I now wonder
What is the rush?
Mind you I have learned something,
The minute I have patience
For something, it comes
Ten times faster.
Now isn't that odd?
On the other hand,
For crying out loud,
Just
How long
Do I need to wait?

Chapter Twenty-Nine

"I didn't see Sneaky for quite a while after his last visit, which was just fine with me because I was starting to burn out. My son came to stay with me over the Christmas holidays which gave me a break from the whole routine."

"I thought your son was living with you?" Neena asked.

"He was, but there were some problems and he was getting into the wrong crowd, so I thought it was best if he lived with his mom for a while. That was long before all this other stuff started happening."

"Were you still trying to do the bets?" Danny asked.

"I was, but it was kind of on and off. I was trying to spend some time with my son. The results were getting very sporadic. One day I would be right on and the next day I'd be off by a mile. I spent a lot of time trying to figure out how to change my thoughts and beliefs about being able to win. I had made enough money to get over Christmas so I was OK that way. The bottom line is that I had worked very hard at trying to win and working with Love, but I was getting very frustrated and needed a break. One day I saw a program on TV about using a chainsaw to carve wood, so the next day I went out and purchased a small chainsaw. I went down to the river and picked up some logs from trees that the beavers had cut down. I spent the next three weeks either with my son or carving. It turned out to be a very good release for the tension that had built up in me. Also it was the first thing in a very long time that I really enjoyed doing, and I came to the conclusion that perhaps there is more to life than just surviving."

"That was a very confusing time. My whole life seemed to be turning upside down, but at the same time I felt better than I ever had. It's like everything was topsy-turvy and yet I had a sense of inner peace, and I was probably smiling and laughing more in one day then I used to do in a whole month."

"I know what you mean," Neena said. "When there are allot of changes happening in a person's life or inside them there's that mid-point where you haven't quite arrived at the new way of life, yet everything has changed. It's like both worlds are mixed together."

"That's exactly what it was."

"So how long did it take before everything leveled off?" Danny asked.

"About another month. After that it was like I was walking on a cloud. I still am today. Everything just seems to click for me and comes out in my favor. I wake up happy in the morning and go to sleep happy at night. Things still happen and every once in a while something will go wrong, but it has very little effect on me. Whatever goes wrong, I just add Love to it and within a very short time it all turns around and ends up being one of the best things that could have happened."

"What do you mean by 'adding Love?'" Danny asked.

"For example, let's say you lost your job, so you send Love to the place where you were working and surround yourself with Love. Then just take the entire situation and just pretend it's a movie and fill the entire situation with Love, even the thoughts you have regarding the circumstance. Just fill them with Love. The end result will be that you end up getting offered another job making more money than the one you had. And maybe you get a little time off to relax and reflect on life. I can give you another example. Someone that I know wanted to learn how to work with Love. Three weeks later she was in a car accident. The minute the accident was over she decided to send Love into the whole scene surrounding all the people that were involved with Love, the cars, everything, just like a movie that was radiating with Love. This is hard to explain, but if you think about it, you'll understand what I mean. Six months later she married the man in the other car, and today they seem happier than two peas in a pod. As soon as you work with Love and spend some time filling yourself and making yourself radiant with Love, everything ends up having a different twist to it. I can't explain it, all I know is if you keep sending Love everything will just end up in your favor when it's all said and done. That's just the way it works."

"Some people probably aren't going to believe that," Danny observed.

"Probably not, but if they take a chance and give it the benefit of the doubt, the results will be there very quickly. After that, there'll be no stopping them."

Neena looked at Danny and then at me. "Our time is running out. You need to finish telling your story."

I didn't understand what she meant about their time is running out, but I saw the look on her face, which seemed to speak on its own.

Another Day

And so another day ends.
But was it really another day?
Are the days different?
Or is it me who's different?
Where does the illusion start?
And where does it stop?
I wonder!

Chapter Thirty

"I almost forgot to tell you this part. When Sneaky was telling me I could go into my past and send Love to my past selves, I decided to try it. At first I only went back to my very early childhood, nine years and less. The reason I chose that time was because I grew up without parental guidance, which sounds rather strange, but that's the way it was. I had no friends. This gave me a very unique view on life because I didn't have anybody telling me that people can't talk to trees or communicate with animals. Actually it's a very natural thing except that nobody seems to understand that and so automatically they teach their children that this isn't possible. So the only friends I had were the animals and the trees. You'd be surprised how much knowledge trees actually have, especially the older ones. They know more about how the universe works than all the scientists put together. The really nice thing about a tree is they never run away. Unconditional Love seems to be their life or the essence of what they are. I decided that area of my life was a good place to start because I knew he needed some company. The strange thing was that whenever I went to see that child self in the past he could see me. We spent quite a bit of time talking. I told him about things that Sneaky had already shown me."

"How did you get yourself into the past?" Danny asked.

"I just used the imaginary train, the same way I went into the future."

"I kept doing this for about a year, not every day but several times a week. As I moved out of my early childhood and started visiting my past self. As he got older, he didn't see me anymore. I would just take myself to the times that were the worst and surround him with Love. I could see the difference it was making. As I was doing this, my present self was beginning to change. Somehow as I changed, my past changed. I can't really point at anything specific, but I know that it's different than the way I saw it before."

"Wait a minute," Danny interrupted. "If you were going into your past and your past self could see you, how did you look to him?"

"I looked like an angel to him." I answered.

"After our Christmas and New Year's holiday, I drove my son to the bus station to go back to his mother. I'm pretty sure that it was January 4, 1996. It wasn't a pleasant drive. Both my son and I were silent. He didn't want to go and I didn't want him to go either. It was extremely painful, like a piece was being ripped out of me. After seeing my son get on the bus, I drove home. Sneaky showed up when I was about halfway there. I could barely see him and hardly hear what he was saying, probably because of the emotional state I was in. I was thinking of all the things that I could have done better and of all the things I had done wrong to bring things to this point."

"'You know, he's hurting as much as you are,' I heard Sneaky say."

"'Oh, that really makes me feel better.' I said. 'There's nothing I can do about how he feels.'"

"'There's a lot you can do. You'd be surprised how much sending Love can heal.'"

"I thought for a minute and looked at him to try to get him into focus so I could see him better.

"'Do you think so?'"

"'Yes!' he was coming in loud and clear now. 'Even if you never saw him again, you could send him Love. If you do this every day, it will make all the difference, more than you can imagine. You know it's easy to do.'"

"I didn't say anything. I just thought to myself that at least I could try."

"'Let me tell you that if everyone did this with a child, it would change everything. If you don't have a child, you can mentally adopt one.'"

"'What do you mean by that?'"

"'I mean to adopt them in your mind and heart and to make the choice to send Love to this child on a daily basis. No one ever needs to know and people do not need to see this child or know where they might be at a particular time. The Love they send will find them. Sending Love this way every day will do so much. It's indescribable.'"

"I turned into the driveway. 'You mean it will keep them off the streets or out of trouble?'"

"'Yes!' he answered. 'It may not change all the circumstances that they are facing, but it will see them through it and with enough Love they will make different decisions.'"

"I thought about what he said while I parked the car and headed into the house."

"I sat in my favorite chair and lit a cigarette. 'Let me get this right. You're saying the more Love someone receives, the less chance there is that they might act out their anger and hurt someone else?'"

"'Yes. On a conscious level they won't know that they are being sent Love. But on a subconscious level they will know, and the Love will counteract a lot of anger and pain that they may be going through. As an example, they might begin to feel that the whole world is not against them. They may not know why the change is happening but nevertheless they will feel it. Just think of some of the hard times you have gone through in your life. Would it have been easier if you had more Love around you, even if you could not see where it was coming from?'"

"'I guess that makes sense,' I answered. 'I guess it doesn't matter where Love comes from, just that you get it.'"

"'You cannot survive without Love. The imaginary valve that allows Love to flow into you is never totally closed, but at a certain point where it is down to a trickle, things will begin to happen. You will be angry, you will feel a lot of pain, and because as the valve closes it becomes painful in the same way that starving to death would be painful. There are certain places in the world that constantly seem to be at war. Why do you think this is? It's simple: in each individual the valve has closed to such agree that all they can think about is anger, hate, jealousy, and so on.'"

"'What would happen if the valve closed totally?'"

"'You would go insane. The rest depends on who you are what circumstances you are in, and where you are. If you live in a war zone you might make a suicide run for your imaginary enemy. If you live in a quiet place you might commit suicide or walk into a store and blow everyone away, including yourself.'"

Unfortunately Sneaky was making sense. If a person feels loved, he would never do anything to anyone else that might be harmful."

"'Would you like me to stretch your mind a little further or would you like me to leave it at that?'"

"'You might as well go for it. You have my attention.'"

"'If twelve percent of the population of any city would send enough Love to fill the area on a daily basis, there would be so much Love in the air that it would be so peaceful the police would have nothing to do. That also applies for a country or the world.'"

"'Now you're really stretching it,' I smiled. 'Why twelve percent?'"

"'Because Love is the most powerful force in the universe. Everything is created from Love. And that is all it would take to tip the scales. Love grows. Nothing can defeat it, nothing can stand against it.'"

We sat in silence for a bit.

"'You have seen and experienced what opening your heart and radiating Love can do. The same thing applies for sending Love.' he said. 'Imagine what would happen if two people in a relationship were to send each other Love. What do you think would happen?'"

"'It would be incredible,' I responded. 'I don't think there would be words to describe the experience. I think I would most definitely like to try that.'"

"I looked towards Sneaky but he was gone. I went to lay down and started sending my son Love."

I looked at Neena and Danny. "I started sending Love to my son that day and have never missed a day since. I can't even begin to tell you the difference that has made. It's incredible. And I will send Love to him on a daily basis for as long as I live. I don't know where things would be today if it weren't for that little bit of knowledge, but frankly I don't want to know.

So It Is

Shit happens,
But
If nobody says No!
And gives Love
Then it will
Just keep on happening
And then, who's really to blame?

Chapter Thirty-One

"Over the next few weeks I spent most of my time experimenting with Love and working on my bets, which by the way were coming along nicely. I had made quite a bit of money but instead of paying off all my bills I decided to put it away just in case. That probably wasn't a bad idea, except I was doing it for the wrong reasons. It's the thought behind the reason that's important. In a manner of speaking I was betting against myself, thinking that perhaps my success would be short lived again. Saving money is fine but I believe now if it is done out of fear, those thoughts in some way create the very circumstance where we will end up desperately needing it. Later on towards spring that's exactly what happened. I wasn't paying enough attention to my thoughts and how they were creating my reality, and so once again I lost my ability to win. Sometimes it seems I'm a slow learner, but nevertheless sooner or later I catch on."

"But I'm getting ahead of myself." I looked at Neena and Danny to see if they were still with me.

"Over the next few weeks of January and February, Sneaky would come around every second or third day. Mostly we just discussed working with Love and talking about various experiments I tried out. I'll give you an example of one experiment. I had a friend who broke off a relationship with a woman. He came to my place and was totally despondent about this relationship. So I decided after he left that I would spend a few days sending him Love and surrounding him with Love. At that time he didn't know anything about what I had been doing over the last few months. A few days later he came back to visit me. I asked him how it was going because he seemed quite happy and relaxed. He told me that for some reason after he had left my place the last time he was here suddenly he felt a sense of calmness come over him. He said that he just started feeling better and better even though he wasn't happy about the break up, but for some reason a large part of the pain seemed to disappear. His exact words were, 'For some reason I feel better than I ever have. Isn't that kind of weird?' I also decided to send her Love. But unfortunately I have no idea what effect it had on her, but from the things I have seen I'm quite positive it made a difference to her."

"I'm pretty sure you get my point."

"Did you tell him about sending Love and some of the other stuff?" Danny asked.

"No! I decided at that time it was probably best to keep to myself. I did tell someone else though. This particular person was running a small business here in town. As I told him about everything that was going on he became more and more interested and wanted to know how he could use Love in his business. Over the next three months I worked with him on that. We also taught his employees to send Love. This took a little bit of convincing, as you can imagine, but we managed to do it. I also made the stipulation that this had to be secret and no one was to say anything to anybody else."

"So what happened?" asked Neena.

"At first, the only thing we noticed was that everybody seemed happier. Everybody seemed to really be enjoying themselves. But nothing happened as far as business was concerned. It took roughly about six weeks and then suddenly business started to increase, very slowly at first. Then it just seemed to take off, and he ended up having to turn business down because he just couldn't handle it all. The other thing that was really interesting which came up in several meetings we had with the employees and himself and his wife who was also working in the business is that everybody was saying that it had an effect on their lives at home. The topic about attracting other people also came up many times. There was one single woman and one single man working there and both mentioned quite a few times that every time they went out they couldn't believe how magnetic they had become to people, especially the opposite sex. It was pretty apparent that they were having the time of their life."

"So what's happening with this business now?" Danny asked. Not a surprising question, considering that his bar was pretty quiet.

"About a year later he sold his business and moved to the United States to open another business. Apparently that's where he always wanted to go. He also took two of his employees with him. From what I have heard throughout the grapevine, he has about 25 employees and is doing great."

"Why do you need to hear it through the grapevine?" Danny asked. "Aren't you in contact with him?"

"No. I knew that at some point I would end up needing to write about this, and I decided that it was best to keep who he is and what business he and his wife are in a secret, at least for the first few years. So I told him that it was best that we do not maintain contact. They both agreed with my reasoning."

"I don't understand why you would do that," Danny said.

"It's pretty simple. I can go into the future and look at the probable outcomes of my book and the information in it. The outcome is unbelievably fantastic. But there are some people who are going to get confused out of fear that they are being controlled. Love has nothing do with control…actually it's the total opposite. Love is attractive and magnetic. Some people are not going to understand, at least at first, that if you have two businesses you can choose from you will automatically be attracted to the one that is radiating with Love. That's only natural. Which will give you the best service and care the most for you? It's pretty simple to answer that question! Unfortunately, some people are afraid of their own shadow. It won't take very long before you'll see small and large businesses doing it everywhere. I'm not saying that my decision was absolutely right, just that I felt it was the right thing to do and that's really all there is to it. Let's get back to the story because there are some other things you need to know."

"After a couple weeks passed, I noticed that I was having some mood swings. I was extremely happy one minute and then the next I felt irritated or angry. At a particularly irritating moment when I felt extremely grumpy, Sneaky snuck up on me and scared the heck out of me, and I let him have it."

"Aren't we grumpy today?" he observed, as my snapping at him just rolled of his shoulders."

"What the heck was that?" I said. "I thought Love was supposed to make me feel good?'"

"Sneaky seemed to think this was pretty funny and obviously knew this topic would be coming up. I was irritated at the fact that once again he didn't bother warning me."

"Look at it this way," he said. 'Imagine a river, and the water is Love. In the past this river of Love in you was almost dry, and now that you have been working with Love, this river has started to flow again. Now imagine as it has increased dramatically in size it is picking up debris left on the riverbank, like emotions, thoughts, guilt, shame, and anger. In a manner of speaking all these things are being flushed out of you. This is temporary, especially if you continue to surround yourself with Love; just look at the feelings and emotions that are coming up and simply send them Love or in your mind surround them with Love. In a few days it will all be gone.'"

"All of it?" I used my hands to describe exactly what I was trying to say."

"Well, you might occasionally encounter a stump here and there. As long as you don't bury it in the sand again, it won't pose much of a problem.' I nodded to let him know I understood."

"We are now going to say goodbye. It's time for you to sit down and put the pieces together. I know you can do it and you will."

"And he disappeared. I was shocked. I still had a million questions to ask. As I sat there thinking I became very irritated at the fact that he had showed up and dropped a bombshell and then just left. After I settled down a bit I realized that is something that I would probably do myself, and have actually done for various reasons."

"So that's it?" Danny asked.

"No, not at all." I answered. "Actually it's just starting but from here on it gets really complicated. I'm going to need a few minutes to think about how to explain this to you."

"Perhaps another scotch while you think?" Danny asked.

"Why not." I answered, drinking the rest of my tea and lighting another cigarette while I took a few moments to gather my thoughts.

One

When a woman feels loved,
She feels beautiful,
When she feels beautiful,
She begins to feel safe,
And then, she will begin to trust,
As she begins to trust,
She will wait and see.
And when she sees your Love can be trusted,
That's when the Magic starts.

Chapter Thirty-Two

"I must be getting tired or something, because I just realized that I forgot to tell you about something else that Sneaky showed me. It's hard to say whether it's important. I'm going to leave it for a few minutes and go over some other details first."

"Over the years I spent an enormous amount of time studying, trying to figure out how the universe works and how everything is put together. And at that time I had a pretty good understanding of how time works, and that the past, present, and future are the same. I had a pretty good understanding of how everything has already happened, and in a sense we are just moving around in the different probabilities and putting them together in certain ways to create what appears to be a life that is lived moment to moment. Knowing this, I had a pretty good suspicion that Sneaky was not an angel at all, but instead either a future part of myself or a probable part of myself. I wasn't sure which one. Today I understand that a future part of myself and a probable part of myself really are the same. The next few months, or actually the next few years, are very complicated to explain, because when you work with Love, it changes time and seems to speed time up. I don't mean that your life is going to be shorter, because exactly the opposite happens. After you really get into working with Love, you will end up doing and accomplishing more in one week than you would have accomplished in two or three weeks. The rest of the world seems to slow down, and as you watch other people who are not working with Love, they seem to be doing things very slowly. It seems to take them forever to accomplish something. Nothing has changed with the other people; it's just you that has changed. Time is relevant to each individual and is different for every one."

"Now you're probably thinking that as time speeds up for you, the amount of things you do in what appears to be a shorter time period would cause you to get tired or burnt out. But that's not what happens. You'll find that you end up having more spare time then you had before. Of course this doesn't take effect overnight. Other people are going to perceive you differently. They will see how much you accomplish in a certain time period, but they will wonder how you did it because you seem to be so relaxed. To some people it will even seem like you do nothing, yet the work is done."

Taking a sip of Scotch, I asked them whether this made any sense. There was no doubt in my mind that Neena understood.

"It makes sense," Danny said, "but it leaves a lot of questions unanswered."

"I agree, but you're going to have to work those things out for yourself."

"So at that time and for quite a long time after that I was doing quite a few different things and heading in different directions at the same time. Everything that I was working on had its own results, some effect on my life, and also on everything else that I was doing. As an example, I was working on my bets, and all the things that I was learning and experiencing with that was a story by itself, one that has no ending. I was working with the people that were putting Love into their business. I was working with time and probabilities; I could write three books on that topic alone. My son came back to live with me and I was using Love to change all the circumstances with him. So many interesting things happened that I could write a book just about sending Love to my son. My ability to hear people's thought was increasing dramatically. That alone would be enough to keep anybody busy for quite a while. This may not necessarily happen to you. It can happen if you want it. The ability to communicate with animals can increase to a certain extent depending on where you were before you started working with Love. I also had a physical life to live. All of this would sound like I was going to put myself into the grave, but it's been the best time of my life. Even though there were difficult moments, it all clicked into place with little effort on my part other than spending a lot of time thinking about everything and working out the details. So this leaves me with the problem of what to tell you about and what to leave alone for now."

"That's easy," Neena said. "Just explain it like you would about a vacation, just go over the highlights. The rest will fill itself in, especially if it's written in a book, because people will have their own experiences."

"That's a very good point."

Desire

She had asked to be
Cherished, but equal.
I said, impossible!
She asked why.
I answered, I don't know how.
So glad that she proved
Me wrong.
And the dance begins.

Chapter Thirty-Three

"Are you going to tell us the piece you had forgotten about?" Danny asked.

"Yes, I think I will." I said, "I haven't put all the pieces together yet, but I think it's going to be a big piece of the puzzle. People seem to think that we're alone on this planet, and that's not entirely true."

"It was before Christmas when this started. I was talking and joking with Sneaky about having a vacation when he suggested that it might be a very good idea. He said the he was going to show me a very interesting place. I figured that he would be taking me somewhere physically, but that's not quite the way it worked out. A couple of days after that conversation I was returning from what I now call my out-of-body train ride, which is probably not the most accurate description since it's only my consciousness that temporarily leaves my body and present reality. I had just gotten back on the train and was looking at the sports results in the newspaper I had picked up when Sneaky decided to make a short appearance. He told me that he was taking me to the vacation spot he had promised. I wasn't all that impressed because I was hoping for something more physically real, but I agreed regardless. When my imaginary train came to a stop he suggested that I go out, and at that moment he disappeared."

"At first it was difficult to clearly see the place where I had arrived, but I have been there many times since. Each time it became clearer and I was able to focus on the surroundings more clearly. It is a fantastically beautiful place. There is a small pond. The water was perfectly clear and every now and then I could see a fish swimming around. Tall grass and patches of wildflowers surrounded the pond. I had not seen many of them before. At one end of the pond there were some trees which appear to turn into a very deep and dense forest. The plants, grass, and trees were not familiar. Sneaky never told me where it was, but he did tell me that it was a real place and that it actually existed. It was quite a few months before I figured out that it was in Hawaii. I haven't figured out exactly where it is on the map but I intend to find it, for various reasons. The reason I didn't recognize the vegetation was because it is in Hawaii. I used to go there a lot but I don't go much anymore because I'm fairly busy with other things, but at that time it was a perfect place for me to go and calm my mind. Many times while I was there, they're was a particular deer that used to come around and lay down beside me. I called her Bambie. Deer have very beautiful eyes, but what I most enjoyed was watching her ears. They were almost like radar dishes that could swivel all the way around. I thought that was the neatest thing. After I had been there a few times I was starting to get the feeling that I was being watched. As it turned out, I was right. I came to the conclusion that whatever was watching me was somewhere in the trees. I asked Sneaky about this several times but each time he would only smile.

One particular time that I was there, the pond was completely still, almost like a sheet of glass. I was watching Bambie when I noticed that there were ripples in the pond, like someone had thrown a small pebble into the water. As I looked at the ripples I noticed that there was something standing partly behind a tree. As I looked directly at it and tried to focus my vision as clearly as possible, it moved away from the tree and closer towards the water's edge. It looked human, but it moved about ten times as fast. I was getting a little nervous but I noticed that Bambie had also seen it and didn't seem to be alarmed. I turned my attention back to whatever it was that was watching me and Bambie. Even though I couldn't see very clearly, it was female, or at least seemed to have female features. She seemed to be wearing something that was made of tree bark. I thought it was some kind of a tree elf but that did not seem to fit. I looked back towards Bambie to see if she was still watching. Bambie's ears were turned in that direction but she was not paying much attention. Before I turned back to the female on the other side of the pond I mentally sent a message that said 'my trees, my lake, go away!' As I looked across the lake I could see she was gone. In the same instant I realized that she was sitting at my left side. That was a shock because I could not decide if she was ugly, beautiful or scary. I have never seen anything like it before. She was looking towards me but not directly at me and did not make direct eye contact. In what seemed like a soft whispering voice that you could have heard for miles, she said, "What makes you think these are your trees?"

There were too many thoughts running around in my head to answer. I just stared. There was nothing about her that looked dangerous, but at the same time I didn't think she was anybody that I should be messing with. She had pointy ears, slightly longer than what would be considered human. Her hair was like soft tree moss. Her skin reminded me of soft paper bark. She had long fingers and long fingernails. Her body features where relatively close to human and she was partly covered with what looked like tree bark cut into thin slices and then hung from her body in different lengths and partly draped over her shoulders. She was slender and about 5 feet tall. Her face was slim with large dark round eyes and large eyelashes…almost like Bambie's eyes. Appearing at the wrong moment she could easily scare the pants off of me but as I continued to look at her I realized she was actually quite beautiful in her own way. She had a scent about her like honey and pine branches and flowers mixed together. Any perfume manufacturer would die for this. Her scent was so enchanting that I had several stray thoughts. I assumed that she had picked up my thoughts because she had a definite smile that would have embarrassed me if she hadn't turned her eyes towards mine. The second we made eye contact I seemed to melt into the universe. I felt like I was one with every tree that has ever lived. It was actually too much for me and somewhere along the line I must have passed out because when I regained consciousness I was back in my bedroom. The next time I saw Sneaky I asked him about her but he refused to tell me anything."

"Over the next six months I went there quite often. Over those six months I learned a lot from her. We spent of time talking mentally. As it turns out there are more of her even though she is the only one I have seen so far. She told me that small groups of them live in various parts of the world. She seemed to know a lot about me and about my life. When I asked her about this she laughed and explained to me that they had known me since I was very little. When I was very young I used to spend a lot of time around a small pond. People always said this pond was haunted. This makes perfect sense considering she told me that there is a small group of them living right by the pond. This pond is right in the middle of a fairly large and old forest. There was a small group of trees that seemed like they were too far apart and almost looked like somebody had planted them in a certain shape. She told me that that is where they have their village. I remember that place very well because whenever I went there I always had the feeling that there was somebody standing beside me or behind me, but I could never really see anything. I asked her why we wouldn't be able to see them or their village. She told me that their vibration is one notch away from ours, which makes them invisible to us, and also we can walk right through them and not feel anything. They can see us because our physical nature is more condensed then theirs, but they are very close to our vibration. I asked her why Sneaky would have brought me here instead of the old pond where I used to play. She said that because of the volcanoes there's a lot of energy around the islands and if I physically came here at a certain point in my life I would most likely be able to physically see them."

I stopped talking for a moment and thought about what I should mention and what I could leave out.

"If I want to go there, would I be able to?" Danny interrupted my thoughts.

"That's very easy to do. All you need to do is exactly the same thing I did: just use your imagination and have your imaginary train take you there."

"But I don't know where it is."

"You don't need to actually know where it is. Just keep in your mind that it is where you want to go and you'll end up there. What's important is that you surround yourself with Love and make yourself as radiant as possible, otherwise they won't appear. They most likely won't take you to their village but someone will come and talk to you."

"Why won't they take us to their village?"

"There are many reasons but none of them have anything to do with fear. If you are radiant enough with Love, they would probably take you to the village because you would be vibrating at a closer range to them. But you won't see much there anyway because they live very simple lives. Actually if you carefully look at the placement of the trees very near the pond, you'll see an area where the trees seem to have a different pattern. That's where the village is. Surprising enough you might even notice that people will avoid this particular spot or not even see it."

"So when are you going?" Neena asked with a smile.

"Within two years, if everything goes to according to my plans. I was planning to get a small house on the beach so I can be near the dolphins. Apparently these people are tied in very closely with dolphins and whales. It's too long a story to get into right now, but the bottom line is that the dolphins and whales are leaving. I've known this for quite some time, and she confirmed it. If enough people don't start to send Love at least several times a week, in less than fifteen years you can kiss them goodbye. That's all it boils down to."

"Allot of people want to do something, but don't know what to do." Neena said. "If you don't write your book, no one will ever know what they can do and what they're capable of accomplishing."

"I know that." I answered. "I've thought about it quite allot. I guess I'm unsure of whether anyone is going to believe it or even give it a chance so that they can see the results for themselves."

"There's only one way to find out, isn't there?" I nodded my head.

Openly trusting

I've thought a lot about trust lately, partly because something has come up, that has touched that part of me that I keep so well hidden.
I wonder what it is that I'm afraid of?
I wonder if I have really ever trusted, or if it was nothing more than a temporary illusion.
I've thought about how many wonderful things I have destroyed because of my lack of trust.
There is nothing in life that I have ever come across that I couldn't handle, yet the question remains: why am I scared?
No relationship works without trust regardless of whether it consists of friendship, Love, work or play.
It comes down to the same thing, trust.
Maybe it's really myself that I don't trust.
Do I trust myself, that I will pick the right whatever?
Possibly? Maybe? After all, who knows what's right for me better than me.

I've heard it said that if you do what is right for you, that is selfish, but I know that if you don't do what is right for you then that becomes destructive.
So where is the balance?
And what will happen to me if I just say the hell with it and just trust?
Perhaps it's whom I trust?
Well that didn't work, did it? It appears I'm right back where I started.
Well, that leaves me with one choice, doesn't it?
I hope that it's not going to be as painful as my lack of trust has been.
On the other hand, Ladies First!

Chapter Thirty-Four

"I was just thinking…" Danny interrupted my thoughts.

"The part about sending Love makes perfect sense to me. Even though I don't really know exactly how it works or precisely where the Love comes from, I can see that it would work and probably work extremely well. But the things you were saying about time and probable events and everything supposedly happening at once doesn't make any sense to me."

I understand what you're saying. I look at things this way. When I learned something like sending Love, at first I'm not interested in exactly how it works but only in two things: that it works, and how to do it. So what I do is temporarily accept the possibility that it works and what I can use it for. Then I accept the possibility that I can do this, because if I spend all my time trying to figure out how it all works, it would take forever and in the mean time I would not get the benefits of what I just learned. I've found that as I use a little trust and move forward with certain information, the information on how it works seems to come forward little by little on its own. This means that I don't have to fill my mind with concepts that are very difficult to understand. That's why I was telling you before to break everything into small units like little jigsaw puzzle. You have one piece of the puzzle that says you can send Love, and you have another piece of the puzzle that says you know how. And if you use those puzzles, soon you will have many little pieces that each tells you what the results are from sending Love. When you put all those pieces together a picture will form in your mind and slowly you will understand how it all works. What's really important, is that you understand everything about Love, or that you have the ability to use it to make your life and everything around you more beautiful?

Neena interrupted. "I think what Danny is having a problem with is the way that you describe time and probable moments. You didn't really put those concepts into small packages like you did with Love and the betting. Do you see what I mean?"

Danny nodded his head in agreement.

"I think so. I can put it into small packages that you can change slightly and temporarily accept so that you can make use of the information to improve your life."

I thought about it for a moment.

"There are books out there on the market that make a great effort to explain the whole concept of how everything actually works. But that would take me forever to explain. It's something you can pursue if you want. I'm not finished with my own learning. It's something that just keeps on going. Every day I add a new piece to the puzzle. So here's how I have broken the pieces down. First I accept that I consist of a conscious mind and a subconscious mind. There also seems to be an inner self, which is like having another deeper subconscious mind. Then there is what I call my soul, which consists of everything that I am. So that's one piece.

Next I take time and separate it from everything else so that it almost is a thing in it's self. Time takes single moments, like a film that is made up of many single pictures, and creates the illusion that one happens after another."

"Then I take a piece that says my soul lives in a timeless way where everything happens at once, or in a sense has already happened."

"Our thoughts create the reality that we live in. What I have done with this is temporarily accept that when I focus on certain things and truly believe that this is the way it is, or truly believe that this particular thing will happen, then either my inner self or my soul puts that into my physical life experience. As I put the pieces together they begin to say that my past, present, and future are all happening at the same moment; it just appears to be different from my viewpoint. This means that I can move forward in time and spend time with my future self because in fact he exists at the same moment I do. There is one more important piece that is hard to accept, but you can use it to your advantage. Let's say you decide whether to go to the movies or stay home. Now two possibilities exist and you must make a decision about which one you will experience. You could stay home and put yourself into an altered state of mind and shift sideways in time and experience both."

"I know this is terribly confusing. To be honest, there are many times it still boggles my mind, but I have gone far enough with it that I can use this information to change my life totally and to create the experiences that I want to physically experience. You can instantly create things that you want depending on whether you believe it's possible. If everything you thought about was instantly created, that could really turn out to be one hell of a nightmare, so our beliefs form a buffer."

"Well, even though I am now more confused, I can temporarily accept that. But I don't understand how I'm going to use it. Let's suppose I want to have a new job. What would I do to make this happen?" Danny still looked uncertain.

"That's the easy part. I do this every single day as soon as I get up in the morning, before I do anything else. I sit down and write out exactly what I'm going to experience today. I don't go into detail, but I write about one page. This took a short while to take effect because I had to create the belief that this would work, but after about 20 days it really started kicking in. So after I write what I want, in my mind I accept it and then form a picture of it. What I picture is exactly what I have written and the feeling that it gives me. Then I simply pump an enormous amount of Love into this picture. I pump as much Love into it as I can possibly fit until I feel it's ready to explode. Then I just let it go and watch it unfold as my day goes along. Some things happen instantly, so fast that it makes my head spin. Other things seem to take a little bit longer but I just work on them every day until they show up. I keep a small diary of things that I experience every day. If you were to look at the two of them you would notice how beautifully they match. The bottom line is that it's really not important to know exactly how it works, just that it does, and that I know how to make it work. There are other ways to do the same thing but the real secret is adding Love, because when you do it with Love. Most of the time it comes out way better than expected. Everyone else associated with it also comes out ahead. Love seems to take the winner/loser issue out of every situation and somehow everyone seems to win. I have absolutely no idea how the Love that I send into what I have written gets into my physical reality, but at this point I'm more interested in the fact that it works."

Relationships

Relationships are simple
Before you say anything or plan on doing anything, ask,
"Will this bring me closer"
Create a feeling of oneness and Love?
If so, it is good
If not, ask yourself
"Why am I destroying this?"
The answer of a thousand failed relationships
Will sit before you.

(We can discuss, debate and argue about everything but it basically boils down to only this)

Chapter Thirty-Five

I stood up. "I need to stretch a little."

I looked at my watch to see if it had started working again, but it was still stopped. I could still see drops of water under the crystal. I was getting very tired and could feel my face slowly starting to relax and droop a little. Danny was looking rather tired himself. Neena looked as fresh as a spring chicken. She must be a night person, I thought, as I stretched my arms to increase the circulation.

"There are some things I don't quite get yet," Danny said. "Apparently Sneaky isn't an angel. Is that correct?"

"That's right." I sat down again.

"Okay, then he's your future self," he ventured.

"I guess you could say that. That's what I thought at the time, but let's just say that time only exists in the physical reality that we perceive. For right now, I've temporarily accepted a new idea that there really isn't any future or past part of myself; they are probable selves. I've noticed that as I play with shifting forward and backward in time, I don't always come across the same past self. It's like the past has had many probabilities and there were countless choices. The bottom line, at least the way I see it now, is that all the possibilities have been lived, and it's like we're replaying the different moments in various order."

I realized that I was getting off track again.

"It's probably better if we just talk about it as past, present, and future selves. Otherwise, it just gets really confusing."

"Why would your future self come back pretending to be an angel?" Neena asked.

I could see that she already knew the answer.

"Because he has a sick sense of humor. It was rather fun, and when and if it becomes my turn to do this type of thing, I will probably do the very same thing. Which makes sense, since he is me and I am him."

Danny asked, "What happened next?"

"After Sneaky left, I took some time and thought about everything. I tried to put it into prospective and in some way tried to get my mind to understand it all. I was curious to know exactly who Sneaky was, how far in the future did he come from. I also wanted to know what was going to happen to my life and me over the next few years. So I was preparing myself to spend a few weeks moving into the future. I wanted to go back to the future self that I had seen sitting on a lawn chair by a cabin, before all this really got started."

I fell into deep thought trying to decide what the best way would be for me to explain this.

"What did you end up seeing?" Danny asked.

"Before I answer that, I would like to say that this didn't all come about in one day. It actually takes a fair bit of effort and concentration and can be very exhausting. Over those few weeks I didn't spend much time betting or working with Love."

"First I moved forward only a few years, but I can't tell you exactly how many; perhaps it was three or four years. I ran into a future probable self who was spending some time in Hawaii. He wasn't very talkative, but he did tell me that he was there working with the dolphins. It appeared that he wasn't alone but he wouldn't tell me who he was with. He just told me that if he said too much it would ruin our timeline and we would and up creating various new probabilities. I didn't understand what he meant, but he told me that it would all start to come together fairly soon and that my main focus should be working with Love."

"The next successful attempt was a strange one. I had many attempts that were not successful. Either I would fall asleep or just end up dreaming. I managed to go back to the same future self that I had seen the first time. I saw my future self-sitting on a lawn chair in front of a fire pit and Sneaky was sitting on a lawn chair at his left. The minute I arrived, Sneaky disappeared. At the same moment I thought I saw a woman dashing into the house. I stood there for a few minutes looking at my future self. He didn't look much different except for having a ponytail, which wasn't anything that I was planning to do as my present self. I also thought that I could see someone peeking through the window but I couldn't make out who this person was."

"I asked my future self, who was just sitting there smiling and staring back at me, where Sneaky went.

"'He's shifting into other probabilities and doing the same thing he did with you," my future self replied. "He was just sticking around to make sure that you would make it this far.'"

"'So he's not really an angel then.'"

"'No, he just has our sense of humor. He was trying to spare you the agony of having to look at yourself completely. I'm sure we can agree that isn't always the most pleasant experience, is it?'"

"'What happens now?'"

"'You need to write about all of this and explain all the different things a person can do with Love.'"

"'That's not going to be very easy. It's going to be almost impossible to get people to believe that something so simple can have such a powerful affect on their lives and on everything else.'"

"'We've already done it. All you're really doing is re-living it in a slightly different probability form.'"

"'If it's already done, why do I need to do it again?'"

"'Because it's not done in your probability.'"

"'Then you're not really my future self?'"

"'Yes and no. We're the same thing. I can be a future self in your probability or I can be just a probable self. But that's not important right now. What you need to focus on is getting as much experience with Love as possible so that you can relay this information to others. The rest will fall into place later on. You also need to concentrate on creating everything that you want to experience in your life. You need to learn how to do this with Love so that everything you create in your life is not only filled with Love but actually created from Love. Do you understand the difference between an object that is created with Love and an object that is created with blood, sweat, and tears?'"

"'I understand that…Who is the person that ran into the house?'"

"'We decided that it was best that you wouldn't see who she is for the moment,' he answered. 'But you'll understand why later.'"

"I was beginning to drift and felt I couldn't stay there much longer, so I asked one last question."

"What happened with the lottery thing?"

"'Forget it,' he said. 'There are better ways to use Love. You'll see what I mean.'"

"He continued to talk, but I had already begun to fade out and moments later lost consciousness."

I rubbed my eyes. "That's really about it. Since then, I've spent most of my time working with Love, which has been quite an experience. The same question remains: how am I going to write about this? Where do I start and where do I stop? It never really stops. Every day I seem to learn something new about sending Love and experiencing new things. And who's going to believe something this bizarre?"

"Write it exactly the way you told it to us," Neena said. "As far as whether anybody believes it, that's a decision everyone needs to make for himself."

"But isn't it too confusing and mind boggling?" I asked.

"That's what makes it interesting," Danny said. "It gives a person something to think about."

"I agree!" Neena said. "But maybe you could write about some of the experiences you had working with Love and some of the different ways you send Love."

Danny nodded his head in agreement.

"You might be right." I said. "I need to go to the washroom. I'll be right back."

I pushed my barstool back and headed for the washroom. I didn't really need to go. I just wanted a moment to myself.

I put down the toilet seat and sat down. I was thinking about what we had talked about, when I noticed that there were voices coming from the bar. I thought maybe a group of people had come in for a drink, but ignored it. After a few more minutes of deep contemplation I got up and washed my hands. As I stepped out of the washroom, I couldn't believe what I saw. There must have been at least ten or twelve people in the bar. Walking towards where we were sitting just moments before, I saw that Danny was no longer behind the bar, but there was someone else there. Neena was also gone and there was a woman sitting in her chair talking to another woman sitting beside her. My chair was still empty. As I stood behind my barstool with my hand on my jacket, I must have had a very confused look on my face. The bartender came over and said that Neena and Danny had to leave.

"What can I get you?" he asked.

I thought for a moment and quietly answered. "Maybe just the bill."

"The bill is taken care of," he reached under the counter. "Danny left something for you." He placed the little green bottle on the counter.

I reached for the bottle and pulled my jacket off the barstool. I was about to reach for my cigarettes but they were gone.

I thanked the bartender and, taking one last look around, headed for the front door. About the same time I stepped onto the sidewalk a cab pulled up and stopped. I opened the door and gave him directions to my house.

The cab driver and I didn't speak much on the way home, but I remember him remarking, "It's a strange night isn't it?"

"It definitely is." I left it at that.

Changing to a Probable Reality

Every time a decision is made,
A whole universe is created where the decision is played out.
In fact, it already exists and since time is not linear,
Any decision can be reversed,
As if it was never played in our reality in the first place.
It is so easy to do,
That every one does it constantly in an unconscious way.
At the moment when a decision is made,
We enter that probable universe and reality
Where that decision is played.
It's not only decisions that cause the shift.
But also thoughts and what we believe.
As an example, if we think and believe we are unloved, that is the probable
reality we are flung into.
And there we will stay until we change our beliefs,
Or until someone comes along who makes us change our beliefs and
thoughts,
But that will never happen until we shift into a loving reality.
Which we cannot do, until we change what we believe and think.
And so we go in circles,
Forever experiencing the same end results.

To Change the Reality

First we must detach what we see, hear, and experience
From our thoughts and beliefs.
That will begin to release us from the probable universe,
We are experiencing now.
Then we change our thoughts and beliefs,
To the point that we experience what we want in our minds.
As the thoughts and beliefs begin to take hold,
We begin to shift.
At first the shift occurs unnoticed,
But as time goes on and with practice, we can begin to see the shifts.
Or perhaps if we choose, we can wait until
Scientists discover a mechanical way. That's if we live that long.

I've heard it said that if we truly believe
In whatever, then we would already have it.
Then it is because we don't believe
That we do not have it,
And perhaps our thoughts are not in line with what we want.

Chapter Thirty-Six

By the time I got home that night I was exhausted. I made something to eat and then went to bed.

I got up fairly late the next morning and after taking a shower and having breakfast I decided to take the bus back downtown to pick up my car. I thought about the night before while I was sitting on the bus. The odds of something like that happening are pretty slim. The whole thing was played out perfectly, like a play that was rehearsed for months. And I fell in hook, line, and sinker. I wondered who Danny and Neena really were, and how could they possibly know who I am. Perhaps one of my future or probable selves knows them and sent them to help. But that still leaves the question as to how they would project themselves into my reality, exactly at the right moment.

I had to walk a few blocks to my car and that gave me a chance to clear my mind. I decided to drive down the street where Neena's bar was and take a look at it during the day. I had been down that street many times before and never saw that bar there before.

It's a one way street, so I drove several blocks further down and then drove back towards where the bar had been. As I got there, I pulled over to the side because there was no bar, just two very large buildings side by side. I couldn't believe it. I know where I had been last night, no question about it. I decided to park my car and retraced my steps. I asked several people if they had heard of Neena's bar. No one had ever heard of it before. I looked in the phone book but there was no listing. That bar doesn't exist in this reality or at least not at this moment.

Even today I still don't really have an answer. All I can say is that perhaps these people know how to shift around in different probabilities and are obviously quite good at it. Or maybe I shifted into their probability. I don't remember doing anything special that night that would cause such a thing to happen. That would be an interesting thing to learn how to do. I haven't stopped looking for the answers and I never will. At some point I'll figure it out "it's only a matter of time". Maybe I'll do it yesterday.

Now as far as Love is concerned, I have spent as much time as possible over the last few years working with Love and have made a lot of fascinating discoveries. I can't put into words the things that can be accomplished using Love. It all hinges on the fact that as individuals, we have the ability to send and receive massive amounts of Love. In the rest of this book I will go over some of my experiences with sending Love and some of the different ways I do it. Sending and working with Love can be one of the easiest things you ever learn to do. I believe that is why sometimes people have doubts about whether this actually works. We seem to believe that if we are not struggling, it must not be of much value, but that is definitely not true.

What I have told you in this book is true even though many things were left out so that it would not be too confusing. I don't expect you to believe anything I have written, and to be totally honest, if someone else were to tell me this story, I probably would not believe it myself. What I'm truly hoping is that you can accept the idea that you do have the ability to send Love and in so doing hopefully you will give it a try. Once you see the results for yourself, there will be nothing left to be said.

My life has changed so much that whenever I think back, all I can do is shake my head. In the past, nothing ever really worked out for me. It seemed like everything I touched turned to dust. Now it's exactly the opposite. I couldn't make a mistake if I tried. Everything I touch works out perfectly; my timing is perfect. If I want something, I type it out on my computer, then I simply fill the idea with Love until it is bursting at the seams. Then I just sit and wait, or follow my instincts about where to go and what to do, and what I wanted falls into my hands. It's usually exceptionally better than I had even hoped.

I have had other people try this and it has worked for them to the same degree it works for me, and sometimes even better.

In case you're wondering why you have never heard of sending Love or read anything about it, that's not an easy story to tell and it really is a long one. I'm still working out some of the details. The amount of effort and energy that has been expended in order to keep this information secret is mind-boggling, and in many ways even disgusting. Normally I would be concerned that this book never would make it to the open market, but for as long as I have lived I have had the feeling that I'm not alone. As I write this, I can feel something looking over my shoulder. I have no idea what it is, but I feel safe and unstoppable, at least as far as this material is concerned.

And so it is. Accept what you like and leave the rest.

All my Love to you on your journey. Why not do it with Love? We have nothing to lose, and everything to gain.

And the game goes on…

Epilogue

The Instructions

Introduction

One concern people seem to have when I mention that we have the ability to send Love to other people is about one person controlling another. Love does not control. There is nothing about Love that is controlling or manipulative. Love has the ability to affect a person's behavior and how they feel. A person who feels Love and is surrounded by Love tends to behave in different ways than one who feels unloved and angry or depressed. When a person is angry, sad, depressed, or feels unloved, his actions resemble the lack of Love. The amount of Love a person has is directly associated with their actions, words, thoughts, and behavior. Normally it is accepted that there is not much we can do, but that is just an illusion. We have the ability to send massive amounts of Love to people, animals, plants, and our environment. The results can be astounding. Children are a perfect example. Their actions are an instant and perfect reflection of the amount of Love they have. Just because someone loves them does not necessarily mean they are receiving this Love, and that's where the difference lies. Loving someone is wonderful but sending them Love is where you will really see the magic.

Who do we send Love to? Everyone, Our lovers, children, friends, co-workers, people we meet, the people who govern our cities and countries, and everyone that you encounter. We can fill our homes with Love, surround our cities with Love, and send Love to our pets and plants. You might be very pleasantly surprised to see how well plants do when they are surrounded with Love. There's nothing stopping anyone from filling an entire field with Love. We can send Love into the food we eat and the food we serve. And on it goes.

Love is very magnetic. It attracts more Love and joy to it. I've watched people change right in front of my eyes and become happier, more joyful, relaxed, and peaceful. It's a wonderful feeling to be able to help others, considering how easy it is. Any place I go, whether it's a meeting, a party, or just a gathering, I always send Love there first, and it makes all the difference. Love is very magnetic and if you fill yourself with Love to the point where you become radiant with Love, you will very quickly find that people are attracted to you and will try to be near you. This is very natural; after all, if you were at a party, who would you gravitate towards? The person who is radiant with Love or someone who is unhappy and not feeling loved? The more radiant we are with Love and the closer people and animals come, the more Love they receive and the happier and more joyful they become. All in all, it becomes an incredible experience for everyone; there is a sense of joy, peace, openness, and belonging.

In order to send Love to other people, animals, plants, or the world, you need to open your heart and let the Love flow. Not only is it as easy as breathing, but each time you send Love you receive more Love yourself because the Love comes from within you and must travel through you before it is sent out. And that's an indescribable bonus.

Opening our hearts and becoming radiant with Love is a very natural thing and happens very often on an unconscious level. For instance when we hold a small baby or puppy or kitten in our arms, our heart begins to open and we begin to feel and radiate Love. When we fall in Love with someone, that other person becomes the trigger mechanism that opens our hearts, but in time the trigger mechanism wears out and then we wonder why we don't feel as much Love as we did before. That's usually when the trouble starts. But when we have the ability to open our hearts consciously by ourselves and send Love to another person, Love can continue to grow instead of drying up like a puddle in the hot sun. There is no limit to the amount of Love people can feel and experience. If we are not in a relationship, we can still feel Love and feel loved. There is no reason why we need to wait day after day for someone to come along to open our hearts. We have the ability to open our hearts, fill ourselves and become radiant with Love and thereby attracting more Love.

When I learned to send Love, it became the joy of my life. For the first time in my life I really felt I could make a difference. What a difference that has made to my life! As I radiate out more Love, I attract more good things and good experiences to myself. The more I work with Love, the more everything just seems to click for me and work out perfectly.

Relaxing and Letting Go

The most important part about learning to open your heart, filling yourself with Love and sending Love, is learning to completely relax and let go of all other thoughts. It's very important during any of the following exercises that you stay focused and leave all other thoughts alone. If you find yourself drifting off, simply bring yourself back and continue. With a little practice and time, you will find it becomes easier each time. Unless you have had some practice with meditation or relaxing exercises, it's probably best that you either lie or sit down somewhere quiet where you will not be disturbed and spend a few moments clearing your mind and totally relaxing your body. With practice you will be able to open your heart and send Love virtually anywhere and anytime, because you will be able to relax your body and instantly clear your mind and focus on your heart.

There's a certain feeling that comes when you open your heart. This is difficult to learn if you do not start off learning it in a quiet and peaceful environment. This is because when your body is totally relaxed and your mind is clear and calm, there is a certain inner sensory perception. This is important because that is where you will find the feelings associated with opening your heart.

Even though I am able to send Love virtually anywhere, like while riding a bus or driving in a car, I still spend 15 to 20 minutes each day where I lie down and totally focus on opening my heart and radiating Love. This seems to dramatically increase my ability every time.

There are many books on the market about relaxing and calming the mind so I won't go into it in too much detail. If you find it is easier for you to relax by listening to perhaps a meditation tape or some very relaxing and soothing music, that seems to work very well and it won't interfere with your ability to open your heart.

Here's what I do whether I'm lying down or sitting. First I totally relax my body by making sure every muscle in my body is relaxed, even my face muscles. I do this by pretending that I'm going to sleep and I tell my body that we are going to have a nap. I let my body go to sleep while I clear my mind of all thoughts. The way I clear my mind is much the same way as the instructions for moving forward in time. I imagine that my mind is connected to the larger part of me. It doesn't matter what you call this part, just connect to it and let all your concerns and other thoughts slip away. I do this by what I call inner listening. I put all my focus and attention on hearing that larger part of myself. After that it's just a matter of focusing my mind on opening my heart and sending Love, whatever it is I choose to do.

If you have a serious problem with keeping your mind from drifting with various thoughts that keep coming up, I imagine an extremely bright beam of light coming down into the top of my head. It reaches directly into the middle of my brain, and then expands from there. This seems to completely clear out all other thoughts.

For maximum results, your body needs to be totally relaxed and even asleep, and your mind needs to be clear of everything except that which you want to achieve. After a bit of practice you will be able to open your heart and send Love anytime, but I have found in the long run that I get maximum results when I lie down and let my body go to sleep while my mind stays awake but focused.

So there it is. It's simple. Sometimes people tell me that they don't have an extra twenty minutes a day for this. I can understand that because they seem to be spending most of their day trying to straighten out all the crap that seems to happen to them. I wonder why so much crap happens to them while my days go by like a lucky charm? Maybe it's that twenty minutes I spend every day sending Love. What do you think?

Opening your Heart, Filling and Surrounding Yourself with Love

Opening our hearts, filling and surrounding ourselves with Love is so easy to do that you'll think it couldn't possibly work, but it does work and it is a very natural occurrence. I pretend there is a valve near my heart in the center of the upper part of my chest. When we fall in Love with someone, this imaginary valve opens, and in a manner of speaking most of the Love we feel comes from us. We also become radiant with Love and as we connect more with the other person we have fallen in Love with, we begin to receive their Love and also send ours to them. As we fall in Love, this other person becomes the trigger mechanism that opens this valve and allows the Love to flow, but in time the things that this person does or says that opened our hearts slowly stops working. That is why sometimes the Love that we felt at the beginning seems to slowly dissipate. As you can imagine, this causes a lot of problems in a relationship. Many times it causes it to end, at which point our hearts begin to close even more, and that is where the largest part of the pain that we feel comes from. As our hearts close it becomes more and more painful. But we have the ability to open our hearts on our own. We do not need to feel the pain that is caused by our hearts closing. We can continuously open our hearts more each day and we can send this Love to each other so that as the days and years go by, we experience more and more Love. There is no limit to the amount of Love we can feel, have, and experience. Many people have told me that as a relationship develops that there is a point where it becomes comfortable and safe. And I agree with that. They have reached an acceptable amount of Love…less than they had at a certain point in their relationship, but more than they had before. But why limit it to that? Why not keep growing further in Love and allowing more Love to grow? Everyone dreams of experiencing more Love even if they have been in a very good relationship for quite some time. It is natural for us to want to grow and to experience more Love each day. And the really beautiful thing about our ability to open our own heart is that we do not need to wait for a relationship so that we can feel and be radiant with Love. It's just a matter of deciding what we really want. Are we totally satisfied with the amount of Love we have or do we want more Love? Why not, it's there inside us and it's free! Where there's an abundance of Love there cannot be pain, anguish, hurt, angers or hate. None of these things can survive in Love. If you have any problems with these other things it's just a matter of opening your heart and filling yourself with Love, and those things will disappear very quickly.

The instructions that follow are very simple, and it's not important for you to follow them one hundred percent. What is important is that your mind is clear and focused on opening your heart, and that your intentions are there. As you begin to play with this exercise in opening your heart, allow it to change to whatever works best for you on that particular day. This exercise is designed to get you started. Let it grow and become you. If you want, you can record the instructions on a tape with some background music and just lie back and follow your own instructions. This actually works very well.

e fun, and keep your pants on because you're not going
.. ᴄʜᴇ things you are going to experience. It's going to be one beautiful ride.

This is how I do it. I lie down because I prefer that to sitting up, but if
I don't have the opportunity to lie down I'll do it sitting up or even standing. I begin to relax my body by simply letting it go.

Next, let go of all thoughts and any concerns you have about things
that you need to do today. Sometimes I pretend that the world doesn't
exist and I tell myself that I refuse to think about anything that is beyond
my physical body.

Breathing properly is also helpful. I breathe very slowly but deeply, taking large slow breaths. This slows down my stray thoughts, and very
quickly tends to bring about a calming effect throughout my body.

Continue breathing slowly and deeply. Bring your consciousness inside
your body. Imagine that you are trying to listen to your inner self or soul
(whatever you prefer to call it). Listen with all your attention, focus on listening and hearing what your inner self might be saying to you. Listen to
the quiet, the peace that is inside you. Continue to do this for as long as
you like.

Now imagine that there is a very bright light in the center of your chest
like a very large brilliant diamond glowing as bright as the sun. Use your
imagination any way you like. See this glowing light as Love. You can see
it as sparkles or a golden light, whatever you choose. Just focus on the fact
that it is Love. Now allow this Love that is glowing from your heart to
become brighter and larger. Use your inner senses to increase the size and
bring it out and beyond your body so that you are becoming a small sun
glowing and radiating with Love. Feel yourself being filled with Love, as
you become more radiant. Notice how every cell in your body is absorbing
this Love and becoming radiant with Love. Feel this Love, feel how you
are now surrounded and radiant with Love. Notice how your hands and
feet are radiating with Love. You are glowing with Love. As you breathe in,
you can feel your lungs filling with Love and even more Love circulating

through your body. Continue to feel this as much as possible. In your imagination, see how radiant you have become with Love. See how everything that you touch receives this Love. Anyone who comes near you receives the Love that you radiate. Continue to see and feel yourself becoming even more radiant, constantly increasing the Love each time you breathe, becoming brighter and more radiant with Love each breath. Feel the joy that is bubbling up from inside you. Feel how you are filled with joy, feel how loved you are. As you become more and more radiant, you are becoming magnetic and drawing more Love to you, attracting people happiness and joy. You are becoming magnetic and drawing good, joyful, and loving things towards you. In your mind's eye see how everyone who comes close to you receives the Love you are radiating. You are so filled with Love that you are radiating Love into the world. Continue to increase the sensation and feelings of Love. You may notice warmth in your chest area, or a feeling of pressure or pain. This is all right. It is because your heart is opening. Keep breathing slowly and deeply, opening to your heart even more. Become even more radiant with Love, filling your entire body and mind with Love. Notice how your thoughts are changing. Notice how you are becoming more loving and understanding as you are becoming Love.

Stay there as long as you want. You can do this as many times a day as you like. The more you do this, the more radiant with Love you will become and the more Love and joy and good things you will attract to yourself. People and animals will want to be near you. Allow them this, for they are searching for more Love and as you become more radiant with Love they receive Love from you. It is a gift beyond words.

Now you can send its Love to other people or fill your home or your work area with Love. The list is endless. If it comes to your mind, send it Love. It's that simple. You have an endless supply of Love. You cannot ever run out.

Sending Love to People

When you want to send Love to a Lover, friends, co workers, or anyone, first you need to open your heart and become radiant with Love, as described in the "Opening Your Heart" exercise. There are different ways you can send Love to other people; each of which has a tendency to give different results. Unfortunately it would take an entire book for me to list all the possibilities that I have seen and experienced, so that is something you will need to discover for yourself. I will explain some of the possibilities.

When you send Love to another person, it's best when we expect nothing in return but are just giving a gift of unconditional Love. It's usually best if you send the Love totally unconditionally; in other words, letting the other person decide in what manner it is best used. Because we are more than our conscious mind, that larger part of ourselves will direct the Love into whatever area it is most needed in the present moment. It is, however, possible to send Love and put a small stipulation with it, as when someone is very ill and you are sending Love to assist their healing. Still in my experience, ninety percent of the time I have found that it is best just to send them Love because sometimes their illness can actually do them more good in the long run than a quick recovery. Sometimes if someone is ill, I will send them Love in various ways, one being unconditional, and also at a separate time send them Love to assist their healing. I do this only if it feels right at the time. When your heart is open and you are radiant with Love, quietly ask which way would be best for this person at this time. You will always receive an answer, most likely as a feeling. If it feels right, do it.

Here are a few different ways that you can send Love. I assume you will know which one will be the correct one at a given time for this particular person.

We can send Love and surround the person with Love, filling with Love the room that this person might be in. This works extremely well in many different circumstances, such as a party that is not going very well. Simply surround everyone with Love and you'll find that the entire mood will change very quickly. This also works well in meetings or job interviews, or even a get-together with a friend. It's like draping them with a warm blanket of Love. And who would say no to that. This also works extremely well if you happen to be with a person who is very nervous or agitated or irritated. You will find that they will calm down considerably and very quickly. In case you're thinking this has anything to do with control, Love has nothing to with control. This is a lot like giving someone a hug, but it's a hundred times more beneficial.

We can send Love directly into the person and filling them with Love, and also send Love to a particular area in their body that they are having some problems with. If you are doing this, imagine the Love going into this particular area in the body and totally filling each cell with Love until they begin to glow and radiate Love. Then visualize whatever ailment they have leaving the body. You can visualize this any way you like. It is your intent to send Love that brings it about. Visualizing it is only the method to engage your intent.

We can send Love directly to a person's heart. This will assist that person in opening their heart and allows the Love to flow into them from their own heart center. This works extremely well if someone has recently ended a relationship or is going through a life crisis and is experiencing a lot of pain. This works extremely well under those circumstances because one of the main reasons they are feeling this pain is because their heart has begun to close. There is nothing more painful.

We can also send Love directly to another person's heart in order to connect more closely with them, such as with your mate or lover. You will find that this creates a very close connection and even allows you to be with that person despite the fact that they may be far away. If two people agree to do this with each other, it can become one of the most beautiful and loving experiences you might ever have. It creates an incredible bond between two people and at the same time you will still be an individual. This sounds like an incredible combination, but it works. And it's beautiful because you will never feel alone, providing both of you agree to this. Timing is not important. Love works beyond time so even if you send your mate Love in the morning and your mate did not do it until the evening, the connection will be exactly the same as if you had done it at exactly the same time. It doesn't really matter how this works. What is important is that it does, and that the results are beautiful.

Open your heart and fill and surround yourself with Love. Then imagine a beam of Love coming from that glowing heart center in your chest, moving upwards to your mind and head center. Now see a beautiful golden beam of Love going from your eyes directly to the eyes of your mate or Lover. Continue with this and at the same time see another beautiful golden beam of Love coming from your heart and going directly to your mate or lover's heart. Be still and continue this for as long as you like. You can also do this at any time of the day and as many times as you like. Remember that Love is unconditional and there are no controlling factors involved here what so ever. When your lover or mate does the same, the connection will be complete even though it is not necessarily done at the same moment. The more you do this the closer you will be connected. I'll let you discover the magic of that, but don't be too surprised if you begin to know what he or she is about to say even before they say it.

So there it is. I'm sure that many of you will discover new things and new ways of sending Love. That's the joy of it. When your heart is open and you are filled and radiant with Love, you will know exactly what to do. Just follow that inner guidance and trust that Love is capable of working its own miracles. All we need to do is give a little.

When I first started with all of this, I used to see Love as a golden sparkling light and I would imagine seeing it go exactly where I was sending it. It doesn't matter how you see Love in your minds eye, only that you have the intention to send Love. I've slowly discovered that using my imagination sends a message to some larger part of myself, which then initiates the process of opening my heart and sending Love. But the bottom line is always the same: it works. When you feel that you have sent enough

Love, stop and continue some other time. You cannot hurt anyone by sending Love, so there is really no reason to be afraid. Have fun!

Sending Love to your Children

I have a child of my own and one of the things that I have learned is that children can be very rewarding but also they can give you challenges that can really boggle the mind. And if you have any buttons, they will push them until something breaks! That is just their nature. The challenge can be quite frustrating sometimes. So in this area I've decided to go into it in more detail because they are our future and our life. If you have children, learning to fill yourself with Love and to send them Love will be one the biggest blessings of your life. I know that's a big statement, but I've been there and I've seen the results.

Around Easter 1996, my son came back to live with me. Everything was going very smoothly, which is saying quite a lot considering he was a teenager. I was spending a lot of my time working on different probabilities and shifting around in those probabilities, and with moving forward and backward in time. This took an enormous amount of effort so I wasn't working much with Love then. I was spending very little time sending Love to my son, which turned out not to be the most productive decision I've ever made. But it turned out to be quite a learning experience.

The only disagreement we basically had was what time he should come home in the evening. This turned into a daily disagreement, and finally it heated up to a very short argument, when my son in his infinite wisdom decided to run away from home to make his point.

I decided to just let it be because I wasn't worried about him because I was able to go where he was, using the same method as I used with Rudy, our dog. This worked extremely well. Unfortunately my ex-wife went into a panic and decided to visit and brought her sister with her. Sometimes the best intentions can do more damage than not, but nevertheless after a few days of running around trying to catch up with my son they reluctantly decided to go home and hoped that he would come back on his own.

I had not told them about my experiences or my work with Love. While they were there I was not able to do the things that I wanted to do. After they left I immediately began sending my son massive amounts of Love. I found one of his friends and gave her an envelope with some money in it, along with a note that said it was fine for him to come home at any time. Then I got on my imaginary train and traveled to where he was and began speaking with that larger part of him. I listened allot, too. Listening was probably the most important part because I began to understand what was going on inside him. I told his larger part that I could give him the freedom that he wanted, but that he should come home as quickly as possible. That larger part agreed. From the moment I began sending Love to him, he was home within thirty-six hours.

When he came home I relaxed my rules about what time he needed to be home. Actually I left it wide open. I have to admit that there was a part of me that was concerned but at the same time there was also a part of me that knew everything would work out perfectly as long as I continued to send him Love.

As soon as my son headed out the door, I took 15 minutes to fill and surround him with as much Love as I could. Within forty-five days everything changed. My son's behavior changed, our relationship changed, the people he was hanging out with changed. It was like I was dealing with a totally different person. It was just incredible. It also would take forever to explain all the details, but you will see those results for yourself.

My son wanted to hang out with a group of teenagers that I wasn't very impressed with or very concerned would be a better way to express it. As I began surrounding him with Love, that all changed. They rejected him even though they would talk to him on the phone and would tell him where they would meet, but when they physically saw him there they would leave him behind. It took me a while to figure out all the details about exactly what happened. When a person is filled and surrounded with Love we vibrate at a different level than someone who is unhappy or angry at the world. We do not match. Look at it from the perspective of the other kids. When he was talking to them on the phone everything was fine because he spoke the same language as they did, but when they met in person, he would be standing there radiating and glowing with Love, and even though consciously they did not see it, they felt it. They would not match and nor would they want him along on their travels.

This caused a bit of confusion for my son because he did not want to be in the goody two shoes crowd but was rejected by the bad boys. At least he was never again in any trouble and things seem to click for him very well. Love is magnetic and so he attracts people to him very easily and people tend to like him very quickly. Something that you may also notice is that when you are filled and surrounded with Love people tend to treat you with a lot more respect and kindness, which is how things seem to work for him now.

To send Love to your children, just follow the same steps as in opening your heart and sending Love to other people. You can also connect to your children using the instructions on how to connect with your mate or lover.

Going where your children are and speaking and listening to that larger part of them is fairly easy to do. It does take a little bit of practice, but everyone can do it. I have made some changes in this over the years. You can take the instructions and record them on a tape, which you can listen to while taking that journey. You can also use this for many other things: for instance, if you want to visit your mate, even if they are out of the country. You can also use this to speak to another person's larger part and very easily solve an argument or a misunderstanding. Remember that listening is more important than expressing your point of view. If you remember that, you will do just fine with it. If you are concerned about privacy, give it up. There is no such thing. It is nothing but an illusion. Think about that and you'll see what I mean. If you're doing things that other people shouldn't find out about, it would be best if you take a second look at those actions, and be prepared to accept the consequences. If there is Love in your heart you have nothing to hide or be afraid of.

By the way, various governments have been using this method for spying for quite a number of years, and it's not even a secret. You can go to any library and look up the information.

To start, follow your normal relaxation exercise and then open your heart, making yourself as radiant with Love as possible.

Now imagine that you are inside a bubble of Love. See and feel this as clearly as possible. Let the world drift away. Begin to think about the person that you want to visit. Don't concern yourself where they might be. Think about them and with your mind, feel your bubble of Love beginning to travel to wherever they are. Your bubble of Love is moving faster and faster. Trust that it will take you where you want to go. Your bubble of Love begins to slow down and as it comes to a stop, the bubble disappears, but you are still radiant and surrounded by Love. Use your imagination to see the person that you have come to visit. Ignore the surroundings. Let them come on their own. Focus only on the person. Is she or he sitting or standing or lying down? Now imagine a beam of beautiful golden Love coming from your heart going directly to their heart, filling and surrounding them with Love, and see Love coming from your heart center into your mind and from your eyes traveling to theirs. Ask a question if you like, or ask them to speak with you and listen. Listen with all your focus but do not strain. Feel the information flowing into you as thoughts, ideas, and feelings. Each time you do this you will be able to hear and understand more clearly.

Continue for as long as you feel comfortable.

When you are done speaking and listening, look at the surroundings. Where are you? What do you see, feel, and sense? Absorb the surroundings; sense them as much as possible. Do this for as long as you like.

When you are ready to return, surround yourself again with a bubble of Love and feel it returning to your present place and time. When you are back, wake up very slowly. If you need to, write down everything you felt, heard, and saw. Have fun!

If you are recording this on a tape, make sure to stretch it out for at least 20 minutes, not counting your relaxation time, and filling and surrounding yourself with Love. I have found that it works best for me after I've gone for a long walk or have done some physical exercise. It's extremely important to allow your body to go to sleep so that all your focus is on what you are trying to do, see, and hear with your inner senses.

Filling your home with Love

At least four to five times a week, I take five extra minutes when I'm working with Love to fill my home with Love. It changes the whole atmosphere of the place and creates a very peaceful and relaxing environment. It seems to remove the normal nervous energy that is in the air, especially in a city. As soon as you walk out my door and off my property you can immediately tell there is a difference. I have yet to have someone visit and not have them mention at some time how peaceful and relaxing it feels. This is not the house or the furniture. When you come to visit, you are literally surrounded and engulfed with Love. Even people who tend to be on the nervous side sit down and calmness seems to come over them.

You can do this no matter where you live, whether it's a house, condo, apartment, tent, cave, or a sleeping bag; it doesn't matter.

It's very easy to do. Before you finish sending or working with Love, imagine that there is a giant valve in your heart that is being cranked open and a massive amount of Love is flowing out. Visualize this Love going everywhere, filling your home and property with Love. Visualize every corner of every room and everything that you have being saturated with Love so that the air is thick with Love. That's it, it's that simple.

Filling your work with Love

This can really be very interesting and a lot of fun. Use your imagination on the different things you can do. For instance, you can fill your work area with Love just the same way you would fill your home with Love. You do not need to be at work to do this. You can do any of these things from anywhere.

I've had of fun with this and have had some fascinating experiences. The most important thing is to open your heart and make yourself radiant. Then you can send Love to all the people you work with, surrounding them with Love. You can send Love to your customers. You can fill the entire business with Love. You can also fill the products you sell with Love. I could easily write a whole book on the experiences I've had with sending Love to my work, but I'll just let you see those results for yourself. Maybe you'll write that book. It will definitely be a book worth reading. They say money talks, but so does Love, and it talks a lot louder. Have fun. And you will, especially once you see how helpful you can be to other people just by sending them Love. One warning: it might be best if you send Love out beyond the area where you work. Otherwise, you may find it will become the local meeting area, and your boss might not see that exactly from the same perspective as you do.

Filling everything with Love

You can add Love to anything you can do mentally or physically, or to anything you touch or think about. There is no end to it. Here's a bit of a list just to get the juices flowing.

Writing a letter? Fill it with Love.

When going for a job interview, why not send Love first?

Fill your home with Love.

Fill your friends with Love.

Send Love to your pets.

Send Love to your plants.

Send Love to your boss.

Send Love to your mate.

Fill everything you have with Love.

Send Love to the animals in the world.

Send Love to the forests, especially the ones that you are trying to protect.

Send Love to the people that are trying to cut these forests down. You might be pleasantly surprised with the results.

Fill and surround your town with Love.

Send Love into the world.

Send Love to the leaders of various towns, cities, provinces and countries. Those results will knock your socks off.

Help other people by sending them Love.

Send Love to your children.

If you are building, carving, painting, or selling something you'll find it will be much more appealing to others if it is radiant with Love.

If enough people send Love into the world and to other people, peace would come about very quickly.

I could go on and on. I'm pretty confident that you get the picture.

A Little Extra Love in the Bedroom

It's always nice and very helpful when you have a partner who is willing to do these things with you, but I know from past experiences that this is not always the case. So if that is the situation you're in, do it anyway for yourself because it will make a difference.

Before making Love with someone it would really be helpful if you take a few minutes and open your heart and become radiant with Love. While you are making Love, slow down and do the exercise for connecting to your partner. Continue to open your heart and send Love directly into the other person's heart. Over time you will find that your intimacy level will go through the roof, and you'll feel more Love than you have ever before. Even if your partner is not interested, it will make a difference for you, and you may then notice some changes happening to your partner.

Sometimes really loving someone deeply can be very frightening, but what is really frightening is never experiencing that deep inner Love.

Creating What You Want with Love

This is very easy to do and will work so perfectly that you'll wonder what's going on. Follow the instructions about opening your heart and becoming radiant. Imagine what it is you want to create. See it in your mind and feel it in your emotions as if you all ready have it. Then send an enormous amount of Love into this scene. Do this every second day until it shows up in your physical reality. Some things will literally show up overnight and other things may take a little longer, but when you get what you want it will be beyond what you expected and it really will be with Love. In case you think this is too simple to work, I can make it more complicated for you if that makes you feel better. The old story about "no pain, no gain" is nothing but a pile of crap, but if you prefer to believe that instead then so be it. And so it will be. It took me many years to learn that and I'm glad I finally got it through my thick skull.

Afterword

Most Asked Questions?

Why was this information hidden? *Some people are obsessed with power and some are afraid of it. That made it easy to hide. Those that are afraid, are so because they tend to believe that power corrupts. I do agree it is what happens many times but not if the very thing that you are using is Love. Love serves to the best of all concerned. It also does not allow anyone to control anyone else and at the same time it releases those that are being controlled and manipulated by others. If you wanted to be in charge and in control of others this information is the last thing you would want those people to know. Neither is it going to be of use to you in that way. Just look at who has been in charge over the centuries and what they have done with their authority. That's why it was hidden, but we with our fears, we help. We are always afraid that someone will have something we don't have and it is fear that causes us to close our eyes to the very thing that will set us free. If you take some time to think about it you will find the reasons for yourself. The point is that it does not matter anymore, the information is here and it's not going to be hidden anymore. Our new technology has created very fast and efficient information transfer that has become unstoppable, unlike in the past.*

One more word! I stated that you could change someone's actions by sending and filling him or her with Love but that is not controlling them. It is simply filling them with the Love that they are lacking and in so doing they will make different and more loving decisions. Also their actions will come from Love rather than from fear, greed and anger, which is where a lot of leaders decisions, are coming from. Not only leaders but also every day people like us. Love changes them not you! But you are the one that gives them that Love for the change to occur. Once you see how well this works you will understand why it was hidden and how.

Is the book true or is it from your imagination? *The book is true. Things happen as I explained them. I did not exaggerate in order to write about it but I did leave some things out in order to make it understandable. I have had some experiences that go slightly beyond what might be believable and felt that it was best to leave them out at the present. It would also have made this book to difficult to understand because so many things were happening at the same time. The rest of the story you'll find in my next book. After you read book 2 you will understand why some things needed to be left out in the first book. If you liked this one the next one will really make the hairs on your back stand at attention. Or if you don't have any you just might, by the time your finished. Just thinking back gives me goose bumps.*

How does Love affect those that would do harm to others? *Love is an energy that sustains all that there is including us. Imagine there is a valve in your body that supplies you with Love. As this valve closes it becomes very painful. It is something that we have become so use to that we don't even know it. But this inner pain is so great that it turns us into people we do not even want to be. Those that do things that we consider bad or hurtful to others their hearts or that valve is very closed only letting enough in to barely survive. It is so painful that they do not have any or very little feeling towards others or the environment around them. Its like having a headache for so long that you don't even know that it is there anymore and do not realize how it is holding you back. It just becomes normal. But it is not. This lack of Love will do many things to people and the effects are wide spread from illness to hate and all* *things in-between. This is where knowing how to open that valve and knowing how to send Love comes in. Sending and filling those people with Love will cause them to change right in front of your eyes. Even if they are on the other side of the world, distance does not matter. You will also find that by opening this valve inside of you that you will not attract hurtful people into your life, they will literally walk around you as if you don't exist. There will still be challenges, which are part of life.*

Are there any side effects to opening that inner valve that opens the Love inside of us? *The only one that I have come across is that if you have been carrying a lot of anger and negative feeling with you. This is what I have experienced for myself. At first it will feel so wonderful that it is impossible to describe, then comes what I call a flushing of old stuff. So what I am saying, is that there will come some old feeling to the surface that has been pushed down but this will pass quickly if you just keep going. Then comes something even more beautiful, which even now puts tears in my eyes from the Love and freedom I feel. Some people feel that I am sticking my neck out saying things like this but I know I'm right and soon you will see it for yourself.*

Why you? Why not someone that is a writer or someone already in the publics eye? I don't mean this as an offense just that you have come out of nowhere with the most amazing information of this century. *I don't take that as an offence I have asked the same question a thousand times myself. I have no answer other than I have a reputation for sticking my nose in places it seemingly does not belong. But frankly my dear I just don't give a hoot anymore. Hope you don't take that as an offence. J*

Are you still playing the lottery? *Very very seldom. I have found much more interesting things to do with working with Love. There is the odd time I buy a ticket but it is either after I have had a dream about numbers or just for the fun of it, if the moment strikes me.*

Sometimes when I send Love an overwhelming feeling of Love comes over me, but other times I feel very little. Why is that? *Why is that? I don't know! It happens to me to. I hope you did not expect me to know everything. I do know that it still works even if we don't feel it happening.*

Conclusions

Today

Sometimes
I wonder about tomorrow.
But then,
That was yesterday,
Or was it the day before?
So what about tomorrow?
Oh, forget it! My Love,
Let's just fall in Love again today...

So that is it for now. Thanks for reading and I hope you have enjoyed it. I also hope that the information will make your dreams come true.

Thank you for purchasing this book and if you have any comments please feel free to email me at the address below.

See web page for email address

Box 40081 Highfield SE, Calgary AB, T2G 5G5

www.livingonlove.uni.cc

www.livingonlove.com

It's a lot of work, isn't it? Well, that's the part of life that really sucks sometimes. Unless you Love what you do or find a way to do what you Love!

Notes

Comments from Readers

Hi Klaus,
I read your book I could not put it down until it was finished. I liked it very much and would give it five stars out of five. Thank you for taking the time out of your life to write it.

G. S.

Dear Klaus:
I am reading your book right now and thoroughly enjoying it. I Love your writing style. It is so honest and sincere. Your Love and deep respect for people clearly comes across in your writing. I like your sense of humor. Humor is important to me as is perspective.

D. D.

Klaus,
I've read your book today and I am so moved. I missed the directions to Danny about how to send Love, but I'm not to the end yet. Wow! Anyway, I am so moved.

K.

Dear Klaus: I just had to tell you I recently read your book...I cried and laughed all the way through!!
My Love and blessings to you and yours,

C.

Klaus, It is a pleasure that you and your experiences have entered my life. I just finished your book and am on the exercises at the end. What a life changing experience. THIS is the missing link. That abundance of Love, now I know that Thanks. This book is an absolute necessity to get out to people.

C.

Greetings,
I just read your Book "Living on Love". I loved it. It rings very true for me.
Thanks,

G.

About the Author

Klaus was born in 1957 at Black Forest Germany. At the age of nine and still with the wonderful idea that Canada was the wild west, where Cowboys and wagon trails still existed; Klaus was sent to live with his Aunt and Uncle in Rosedale, British Columbia, Canada. Although he was disappointed at not seeing the western plains and chuckwagons, he lived in Canada and grew up to accomplish many things. Klaus has been a dairy farmer, contractor, artist, entrepreneur and author.